Oxford Shakespeare Topics

GENERAL EDITORS: PETER HOLLAND AND STANLEY WELLS

Shakespeare's Late Work

RAPHAEL LYNE

OXFORD

UNIVERSITY PRESS

OXFORD
UNIVERSITY PRESS

Great Clarendon Street, Oxford OX2 6DP

Oxford University Press is a department of the University of Oxford.
It furthers the University's objective of excellence in research, scholarship,
and education by publishing worldwide in

Oxford New York

Auckland Cape Town Dar es Salaam Hong Kong Karachi
Kuala Lumpur Madrid Melbourne Mexico City Nairobi
New Delhi Shanghai Taipei Toronto

With offices in

Argentina Austria Brazil Chile Czech Republic France Greece
Guatemala Hungary Italy Japan Poland Portugal Singapore
South Korea Switzerland Thailand Turkey Ukraine Vietnam

Oxford is a registered trade mark of Oxford University Press
in the UK and in certain other countries

Published in the United States
by Oxford University Press Inc., New York

British Library Cataloguing in Publication Data
Data available

Library of Congress Cataloging in Publication Data
Data available

Typeset by Laserwords Private Limited, Chennai, India
Printed in Great Britain
on acid-free paper by
Biddles Ltd., King's Lynn, Norfolk

ISBN 978-0-19-926594-7
ISBN 978-0-19-926595-4 (Pbk.)

10 9 8 7 6 5 4 3 2 1

For Valeda May Rees
and in memory of Thomas Schofield Rees

Acknowledgements

This book is dedicated to my inspirational maternal grandparents, who were much in my thoughts as I was finishing it. Then my father died, as I was revising it—I hope in another book to make an appropriate acknowledgement of my enormous debt to him.

I have been remarkably lucky in my teachers of Shakespeare at St Edward's School, Oxford, and then at Cambridge. The path to this book started, I think, with doing *Macbeth* for O level with John Gidney, and then *The Winter's Tale* for A level with John Trotman. I was supervised brilliantly as an undergraduate by John Kerrigan and Anne Barton. Any or all of these may feel like Dr Frankenstein after reading this book—they're not to blame, but they have my deep gratitude. After that, I became the teacher, and over the last decade or so aspects of this book have been tested and refined by a succession of excellent students at the University of Cambridge, at the University of Cambridge Shakespeare Summer School, and on the University of New Hampshire Summer Program.

One of the few things I have in common with Shakespeare is that I have been edited by Stanley Wells and Peter Holland for Oxford University Press. I'm sure Shakespeare would agree that their humane rigour is a wonderfully improving thing. But of course, they too cannot be blamed for remaining wrongdoings in this book. At OUP Tom Perridge has been consummately patient and assiduous. I'm also grateful for many insights gleaned from conversations with Gavin Alexander, Rebecca Beale, Colin Burrow, Patrick Cheney, David Colclough, Paul Hartle, Gordon McMullan, Subha Mukherji, Jason Scott-Warren, and Tiffany Stern.

Finally, my family have been wonderful. My mother and sister and grandma in particular have been brave and kind as ever. Clare, Thomas, and Sophie have made everything a joy.

Contents

The Late Shakespearian Canon

Nothing of him that doth fade
But doth suffer a sea-change
Into something rich and strange.

(*The Tempest*, 1.2.402–4)

Readers, audiences, and critics have regularly described special qualities in the works written towards the end of Shakespeare's theatrical career: especially *Pericles*, *Cymbeline*, *The Winter's Tale*, and *The Tempest*. Ariel's song, quoted above, calms and perplexes Ferdinand with its description of an intriguing physical change, but as the prince discovers later, Alonso has not actually died at all. While extraordinary stories filled with emotional intensity and challenging dramaturgy add up to a 'rich and strange' new direction in Shakespeare's career, the metamorphosis can be overstated—many key interests of earlier works find themselves reworked. The goal of this book is to explore and characterize new and old features in Shakespeare's late writing. This is a complex but rewarding task: these are elusive, finely tuned works that illuminate the richness and strangeness of fundamental questions about people, society, the supernatural, and the dramatic, rather than offering answers.

Even the question 'what is Shakespeare's late work?' is only deceptively straightforward. There is an easy answer, namely 'the work written at and towards the end of Shakespeare's career'. However, this answer masks considerable complexity. Critics have defined different groupings of 'late' or 'last' plays, the usual tendency being to create tight trios, quartets, or quintets centred on *The Tempest*. E. M. W. Tillyard's classic study *Shakespeare's Last Plays* (1938) covers only *Cymbeline, The Winter's Tale*, and *The Tempest*—the latter being Shakespeare's final single-authored play (though not his last work). He excluded *Pericles* on debatable grounds of authorship and quality: 'although it is likely that the last three acts are mainly Shakespeare, there is no proof that he handled them seriously enough to justify our basing any elaborate theorizing upon them'.[1] In *Shakespeare: The Last Phase* (1954) Derek Traversi included *Pericles* but was no less *Tempest*-oriented as he considered the importance of the climax of that play: 'For it is at this point, if anywhere, that the pattern of *The Tempest*, and with it the whole design initiated in the history plays and carried through the tragedies to the last symbolic comedies here under consideration, is substantially complete.'[2] Traversi's book tries to rescue the late romances from an obscurity they no longer suffer. For him, the group of four plays represents a consummation of Shakespeare's interests and a move towards completeness in a drama that includes the central character renouncing his art. Readers and audiences wonder how much Prospero's renunciation parallels the author's own turn towards retirement; quite understandably, though to do so relies on speculation (in constructing how Shakespeare ended his career) and an imaginative leap. Traversi's canon of four emphasizes this end-point and a coherent group of plays with much in common.

They cohere because they share generic characteristics. To some extent one could say that they share a genre or a mode, and the usual modern term for that genre or mode is romance. This is a rather unstable category and needs qualification. It was not used of Shakespeare's plays in their time. Perhaps the most relevant and rather fashionable term that could have been used then was 'tragicomedy'. This was the term used of plays by Shakespeare's contemporary John Fletcher, and the theory and practice of tragicomedy were, in the early seventeenth century, being translated into English from Italian.[3] However, we do not have evidence of the term being used about any of Shakespeare's plays. The collected works of Beaumont and Fletcher, printed in 1647, were billed as 'Comedies and Tragedies' despite the presence within of some of the most important tragicomedies of the period. In the well-known generic divisions of the First Folio edition of Shakespeare (1623) *The Tempest* and *The Winter's Tale* are comedies, while *Cymbeline* is a tragedy. *Pericles* is not included. Nevertheless the identification of a genre does not depend on contemporary attestation and a brief rehearsal of the characteristics of 'romance' clarifies the connection. Whether it wholly displaces the claim of 'tragicomedy' is not clear: these works do indeed combine the tragic and the comic in various ways, with the endings predominantly comic and the trials and tribulations potentially tragic. However, the advantage of 'romance' is that it captures the manner of the action rather than its content.

Romance has a long history, from the Hellenistic novel, through medieval chivalric poems, and, very pertinently for the late plays, an Elizabethan revival in the wake of Sidney's *Arcadia* (*c*.1580; printed 1590). The romance tradition that bears on Shakespeare has general and specific features that recur in the late plays.[4] Some of these characteristics are the basic ground of the grouping together of the four romances, and some will become important in this chapter's opening out of the late canon, so it is worth outlining them here. Narrative romances often feature heroic personal quests, but the individual quest is not a hallmark of Shakespearian romance. However, there are tortuous voyages towards self-discovery, and the endings of the plays see marvellous discoveries and recoveries of lost things. The difference is, perhaps, that the agency of the hero and the glorious outcome are not so directly related as in many previous manifestations. Shakespeare's emphasis is frequently on other, higher powers, alongside the worth of the heroes. The romance tradition very often has an allegorical aspect, in which the actions and characters signify on other levels, especially on a spiritual level. This is certainly a feature of Shakespeare's late plays, though they are not really allegorical: a supernatural register is never far away, and often intervenes strongly. They are wondrous in two senses: first, they are improbable (and they make an issue of their patent fictionality); and second, they are miraculous in a more religious sense—they bring to mind the actions of gods, and of God.

In romance the structure of searching followed by finding is clearly vital, but some important critics of the mode have concluded that the process of time, as much as the conclusion of the process, is critical. For Patricia Parker, a crucial quality of romance is the tendency to defer endings.[5] Northrop Frye, who considers genres and modes from an anthropological perspective, encounters this aspect of romance as part of a mythological system:

Romance, the kernel of fable, begins an upward journey toward man's recovery of what he projects as sacred myth. At the bottom of the mythological universe is a death and rebirth process which cares nothing for the individual; at the top is the individual's regained identity. At the bottom is a memory which can only be returned to, a closed circle of recurrence: at the top is the recreation of memory.[6]

There are two reasons why it is problematic to approach Shakespeare's romances in mythical terms. One is that these plays are closely embroiled in their immediate historical milieu and cannot be read as straightforwardly ideal or archetypal. Political concerns, and the dynamics of earthly power, are often in evidence. The other is their constant self-conscious quality, and the sometimes light-fingered way they achieve their movement from a 'closed circle of recurrence' to the 'recreation of memory'. Crucially, they manage to sustain both the supernatural and the self-conscious. Frye's description is suggestive especially as a model for the temporally suspended situations of Prospero, Leontes, and other figures from Shakespearian romance. The structure of time in these plays is complex, and includes intriguing suspensions and reactivations. The attainment of the final goal is suitably climactic, somewhat in contrast with Parker's emphasis on deferral. This may be the result of dramatizing romance, in which the physical experience of time in the theatre shifts the focus of romance towards its ending.

Many of these romance characteristics are evident in Shakespeare's earlier work. In *The Comedy of Errors* and *Twelfth Night*, for example, lengthy travels and fractured identities are resolved in final scenes of reunion and restoration. These comedies clearly share many things with romance, and it is important to register these affinities as well as to suggest differences. Shakespeare's late work returns to familiar dramatic territory and transforms it. The romances are more sharply tragicomic than the comedies: threats of death and scenes of suffering are more acute. Encounters with the supernatural are also more direct and emphatic, as in *The Winter's Tale*:

> CLEOMENES The climate's delicate, the air most sweet;
>   Fertile the isle, the temple much surpassing
>   The common praise it bears.
> DION   I shall report,
>   For most it caught me, the celestial habits—
>   Methinks I so should term them—and the reverence
>   Of the grave wearers. O, the sacrifice—

How ceremonious, solemn, and unearthly
It was i'th' off'ring!
CLEOMENES   But of all, the burst
And the ear-deaf'ning voice o'th' oracle,
Kin to Jove's thunder, so surprised my sense
That I was nothing.

(3.1.1–11)

Cleomenes and Dion are returning from Delphi with the oracle's view of Leontes' accusations. It is notable that their experiences have been unexpected. They are truly rocked by what they have seen, and Dion moves only reluctantly towards calling things 'celestial' ('Methinks I so should term them'). This scene is not crucial to the plot of the play, though it does amplify the wrongness of Leontes when he rejects everything in the oracle. However, it has a key function in generating the atmosphere of romance. Here we see two characters forcibly engaged with a world beyond theirs, ensuring that the events of the play are to be interpreted within or alongside such a grand register. In Shakespearian comedy there is not such an emphatic heightening of the atmosphere: the mortal world of the play is quickly regained.

The reunion scenes of the romances differ from those in the earlier comedies in a similar way. Surprises tend to accumulate in greater numbers, but more importantly they unfold with a greater degree of numinous wonder. These grand marvels and powerful emotions develop alongside the complexity and anxiety that accompany comic resolutions in Shakespeare. There is potential for comic and more serious doubts at the extraordinary and unbelievable things unfolding on the stage. The final scene of *Cymbeline* sees this in action:

BELARIUS [*rising*]   Be pleased a while.
This gentleman, whom I call Polydore,
Most worthy prince, as yours, is true Guiderius.
     [*Guiderius kneels*]
This gentleman, my Cadwal, Arviragus,
Your younger princely son.
     [*Arviragus kneels*]
                              He, sir, was lapped
In a most curious mantle wrought by th' hand
Of his queen mother, which for more probation
I can with ease produce.

CYMBELINE   Guiderius had
    Upon his neck a mole, a sanguine star.
    It was a mark of wonder.
BELARIUS   This is he,
    Who hath upon him still that natural stamp.
    It was wise nature's end in the donation
    To be his evidence now.
CYMBELINE   O, what am I?
    A mother to the birth of three? Ne'er mother
    Rejoiced deliverance more. Blest pray you be,
    That, after this strange starting from your orbs,
    You may reign in them now!

                                    (5.6.357–73)

This is only one of the multiple reunions. As in many recognition scenes much is made of significant tokens: Belarius offers one, the 'curious mantle', and Cymbeline asks for another, Guiderius's mole. When Belarius says that 'it was wise nature's end in the dona-tion'—everything has followed a providential plan—this could just be a bit of conventional piety, but in this play, which actually has a staged divine intervention, and in Shakespearian romance generally, the presence of the supernatural is tangible and pressing. The 'curious' nature of the mantle, and the 'wonder' in the strange mole turn out to be meaningful in their eventual functions. Cymbeline's reaction is, of course, a mixture of joy and astonishment, and Shakespeare gives him a joyful and astonishing way of capturing the feeling: 'am I | A mother to the birth of three?' There are many aspects to this image: it is a truly vivid way of expressing the emotion of the moment; it is a poignant reminder that Cymbeline's wife, the true mother of his children, is long dead; and it is a strange image that brings the audience into contact with the strangeness of the scene. Cymbeline's claim of motherhood could make viewers smile, or even laugh—and many other excessive or extraordinary things in this scene have the same quality. The important thing is that these things cooperate: the absurdity and the wonder and the majesty can all live together.

    This, then, is a central characteristic of Shakespeare's late work: remarkable and substantial things sit alongside notes of humour and scepticism. Much of this book will explore the ways in which Shakespeare makes huge but qualified investments in some weighty

ideas. Chapters 2–5 explore how the romances find hope and consolation in the mercy and grace of God, in the value of family bonds, in
the security and rightness of royal power and the political status quo,
and in the effectiveness and truth of dramatic representation. They
also acknowledge the ways in which Shakespeare questions such hope
and consolation: alongside a passionate encounter with the restorative power of a daughter's love, for example, there is a contradictory
emphasis on the discordant emotions and inhibiting consequences that
can accompany intense family bonds. None of these grand principles
is advanced without qualification, and the nature of that qualification
can often be called ironic.

Irony has a complex history in philosophy that can help illuminate
the profundity of the ironic structures characteristic of late Shakespeare. It is a feature of linguistic exchange: an ironic statement implies
a meaning other than itself. For the Greeks and Romans, and their
renaissance inheritors, it was first and foremost a rhetorical figure.
However, in some literature and philosophy it can seem as if the world
itself is in essence ironic—that the truth is by nature elusive and
must be qualified to the point of being contradictory or self-defeating.
Even the classical version of rhetorical irony is not straightforward or
simple. Socrates in Plato's dialogues employs means of reaching truth
(deceptive manoeuvres, spurious hypotheses) which suggest that truth
itself may be unstable. Renaissance writers and scholars rediscovered
Socratic irony and its possibilities: the brilliant, flexible thought of
Erasmus, Bacon, Montaigne, and others can be connected to this
revival.[7] It still has a large rhetorical component: irony is a means of
arguing and creating a persuasive voice. The presence of an ironic
world-view is subsidiary, fragmentary, and intermittent. As such this
renaissance practice does not provide on its own an analogy for, or
explanation of, the place of irony in the drama of late Shakespeare.
However, throughout the history of thought about irony there has
been a more or less close encounter with a consequence of the Platonic
rhetorical model: when the means of persuasion are so flexible and
elusive, the things proposed—however vital and substantial they may
seem—risk appearing debatable themselves.

An ironic habit of thought tends towards questioning everything. In
the end this tendency may be resolved by something like religious faith,
or it may not. This bears a close resemblance to the structural dilemma

of Shakespeare's late work as it has been set out thus far. The plays posit things in which one might believe, and the ironic tools to doubt them: the beliefs proposed can be weighty enough to transcend irony, but for the literary reader or the theatre audience irony itself is precious. In subsequent philosophy, despite many differences, the shape of irony has persistent characteristics. The overlap between irony as a style of speech and irony as a mode of existence is seen throughout; modern philosophy takes the lead from Plato but supplies less faith in the substance of the truth being revealed. Claire Colebrook's introduction to the subject is particularly useful as it recognizes the special urgency of thinking about irony for twenty-first-century readers.[8] Colebrook insists on the need to value the ultimate goal of the intellectual or spiritual quest, however distant it may seem—without this, irony is a much weaker thing. This also suggests things about the nature of Shakespeare's late work: the fullest reading of these plays, it might be argued, requires both a commitment to the value of family, social order, religion, and the theatre itself, and a willingness to appreciate the full complexity and fragility of these things.

Perhaps the most vivid articulation of irony's power comes in Romantic philosophy; here the nature of reality and an ironic approach to it are intimately connected. Friedrich Schlegel in particular explored how literary irony might be a response to the problems of encountering the world.[9] Individuals are often painfully aware that their environments are at odds with their desires and beliefs. Where one cannot acquire a wholly valid vision of the world, the slippage between the observer and the world that one finds in literature might itself reveal an alternative authenticity. Schlegel argues that literature should recognize its artificiality, and that it should draw attention to problems of authenticity, in order that the reader might fully experience the value of the resultant slippage. Muecke expresses this in terms of the contrast between the 'observable' irony of existence (the problem) and the 'instrumental' irony of literature (a possible solution).[10] Later thinkers—Georg Lukács on the novel, for example, and postmodern critics such as Paul De Man—also attribute representative power to irony, in tune with historical environments requiring yet more new approaches to truth.[11] The repeating theme is that irony offers a way round the essential incomprehensibility of existence, either by truly embodying the paradoxes of that incomprehensibility, or by allowing a different path to authenticity. A key thought underlying much of this book is that the ubiquitous irony of Shakespeare's late work is philosophical, and is part of a tradition of philosophy with enduring characteristics.

Irony in the Renaissance and in Shakespeare has a close relationship to scepticism—the philosophical system wherein doubt is universal. Like irony, this has classical origins and was revived in the Renaissance: Michel de Montaigne, perhaps the philosopher who meant most to Shakespeare, was deeply influenced by it.[12] Graham Bradshaw has considered Shakespeare's own version of scepticism in a very important book. Though most of it concerns tragedies, when it does touch on romance it is highly perceptive. On the final scene of *The Winter's Tale* he says that 'we become aware of our participant roles, find ourselves considering the nature of our own involvement with the "feigning", and find the play we are watching is watching us'.[13] This way of thinking about the play is central to the next chapter. There are numerous affinities between the scepticism of the late plays and their irony: the vital turn taken (and most clearly evident in the context of irony) is that they are able to be constructive despite shedding doubt on the things being constructed.

Alongside scepticism the other key parallel concept is metatheatricality—the specifically dramatic form of irony where the mode of representation is the focus, as it is in Bradshaw's reading of *The Winter's Tale*. This is ubiquitous in Shakespeare, who always keeps the theatrical nature of events in the audience's mind. Anne Righter (Barton) places Shakespeare at the heart of a process of increasing self-consciousness in English drama from the Middle Ages onwards.[14] There is no doubt that metatheatricality is vitally important to late Shakespeare as to all Shakespeare. Indeed, there is so much metatheatre, so many moments where characters act, or comment on acting, or make oblique or specific references to theatrical performance, that it cannot be seen as a repeating in-joke, or a nervous gesture, or a part of his basic technique. Rather, it may be that the philosophical climate of the late plays makes clear what has always been true, that metatheatre, like irony, has a philosophical aspect with a close relationship to scepticism (though not contained within it). Plays invite questions, and when they display and interrogate their own nature, they add depths and problems to these questions and to the status of questioning.

This sense of philosophical seriousness and fundamental irony in combination contrasts with some earlier accounts of late Shakespeare. Robert Sharpe, for example, takes a very positive line on the nature of irony in the romances. He calls them 'his fourth period, of a serenity and tolerance allowing little in the way of bitter intensity, but much in that of a cosmic, almost godlike irony such as Prospero's'.[15] It traces this essential lack of sharp irony back to a change of mood in Shakespeare himself: 'Shakespeare has now made his peace with God and man. He has accepted his universe and has succeeded in finding detachment from even the most torturing ironic paradox, that man is both beast and angel.'[16] The discussion of Shakespeare in this book explores something not entirely unlike this—a constructive mood, open to heightened experience, holding faith in greater things. However, this is accompanied by sharp doubts. Critics who see the late plays as an antidote to the fractures and disasters of the preceding tragedies run the risk of oversimplifying the role of irony therein. For example David Bevington, in a survey of Shakespearian irony, says that 'the saddening ironies of the fallen world in the tragicomedies repeatedly dissolve into cosmic laughter'.[17] But this does not seem like an irony of dissolution: of paradoxical accretion or mysterious juxtaposition, perhaps. Irony in late Shakespeare has many parts: the ironic vision of the world developed in the theory of irony in the Romantics and beyond, the evasive tone that goes all the way back to Plato, a self-conscious defence against excessive sincerity, and a means of creating a response to the world's difficulties. Shakespeare creates imaginative space around the new key ideas, and central themes from his earlier work, and this is the keynote of Shakespearian irony. By being so subtly and persistently ironic, he enables multiple responses ranging from the cynical to the idealistic. These multiple responses are vital in appreciating the bold endeavour of Shakespeare's late work: bold, because grand ideas and hopes are given heartfelt expression, bold also because despite that heartfelt expression there is always freedom for readers and audiences to ask questions.

There are characteristics special to Shakespeare's late work, and these characteristics might well fit with 'lateness' in a literary career. At various points this will emerge in this study, though it is not essential. Both a tendency to try to reach for a source of substance and certainty in the world, and a tendency to recognize the limits of certainty in the light of experience, could suit an author's final phase. One should not overstate this: it is impossible to show that Shakespeare managed his career to this extent, and there is no pressing need to consider these works as anything other than coincidentally 'late'. However, rather than eschewing any thought that Shakespeare's late work makes an issue of its own lateness, this book aims to explore this very feature—but rather than creating a narrative out of closure, it will also recognize how Shakespeare incorporates resistance to any sense of impending ending. The path towards retirement, if indeed such a term is justified given the lack of evidence for any active decision to leave the theatre, was not linear, yet there are numerous tactics and strategies that suggest, paradoxically, the inauguration of a valedictory tone. With this in mind, newly accommodating and permeable boundaries of late Shakespeare need to be addressed. Throughout, the genre of romance is at issue, and the extension of the boundaries of late Shakespeare reveals a broader and persistent interest in the issues aired and explored in the classic restricted canon.

The goal of this study is to characterize and analyse the similarities between the four romances, but also to open up the idea of late Shakespeare and thereby to consider a wider range of works. Paradoxically, such opening up both strengthens the importance of the details of the similarities, and puts them into a more varied context. Previous studies of these works that finished with *The Tempest* constructed a particularly strained form of 'lateness'. Shakespeare's writing continued for at least two more years. The late work is not a closed or stable category, so in the rest of this chapter the principles behind broadening the admissible canon will be explored. *The Tempest* has some climactic and final qualities, but it is by no means the last play Shakespeare wrote. He wrote at least two, and probably three, later plays in collaboration with John Fletcher, his successor as the leading dramatist of the King's Men. *Henry VIII*, *The Two Noble Kinsmen*, and what little can be made from the difficult case of the lost play *Cardenio*, all have qualities that connect with those outlined as the core of the late Shakespearian mode. In Chapter 6 the issues arising from the fact of collaboration in these plays will be central: the alliance with Fletcher turns out to be both harmonious and sharp-edged. The characteristics of the late work, distinctive though they can seem, are closely entwined with the work of other authors and, indeed, Shakespeare's own earlier work.

There is a revealing critical argument that bears upon the relationship between these co-authored plays and the 'four romances'. On one side there are those who see a crucial distinction between single-authored plays (of which *The Tempest* is the last, with its hints of retirement and of artistic completion) and collaborative plays. On the other are those who do not, on the basis that writers of this period did not seem so troubled by the distinction as modern critics. Brian Vickers's book *Shakespeare, Co-Author* makes an emphatic case for the fact of collaboration on several plays, building on and reasserting the work of previous scholars.[18] The role of Fletcher in *Henry VIII* and *The Two Noble Kinsmen* is set out in detail. *Pericles* is shown to be a collaboration with George Wilkins, a minor writer who wrote a prose version of the same story (on which more in Chapter 3). The plays are, in Vickers's account, divided as follows:

Pericles: Shakespeare wrote Acts 3–5
Henry VIII: Shakespeare wrote 1.1, 1.2, 2.3, 2.4, 3.2, 5.1
The Two Noble Kinsmen: Shakespeare wrote 1.1, 1.2, 1.3, 1.4, 2.1, 3.1, 3.2, 4.3, 5.1, 5.3, 5.4.

In this book I shall accept these conclusions drawn by Vickers on the basis of numerous earlier studies of linguistic features. He exposes many expressions of doubt about collaboration as decidedly wilful in their resistance to linguistic evidence. One of the main sources for Vickers is Jonathan Hope's rigorous and judicious *The Authorship of Shakespeare's Plays*. The conventional attributions to Fletcher and Shakespeare are corroborated by analysis of such linguistic fingerprints as the use of the auxiliary 'do' (that is, saying 'I do eat' rather than 'I eat'), and the use of relative pronouns (which, who(m), that, or none at all). Each writer has measurable tendencies and preferences and these turn out to be identifiable in different parts of the plays. Hope's analysis often echoes the brilliant intuitive allocations of earlier critics. The case of *Pericles* is a little more complicated. Hope's evidence 'does not conflict' with the hypothesis: '*Pericles* as we know it is a final draft by Wilkins of a collaboration between him and Shakespeare in which Wilkins contributed more to Acts 1 and 2 than to the remainder of the play.'[19] Hope's careful formulation reflects the problems of the play and the fact that sometimes linguistic evidence is muddied by different kinds of collaboration. Shakespeare and Fletcher share the plays out, more or less, and leave their distinctive marks. Shakespeare and Wilkins evidently did not do that.

Once the fact of collaboration is established, and segments of a play are more or less securely divided between the two authors, there are still problems. Critics differ greatly on how to read the resulting works. For Vickers the difference between authors comes through: Shakespeare's characterization is different and generally superior, his parts of the play more important and more successful.[20] Gordon McMullan, conversely, in his edition of *Henry VIII*, argues that the play should be seen as a complete dramatic experience that coheres in numerous ways.[21] Vickers takes issue with McMullan most vehemently because he cites Michel Foucault in support of his position: for Vickers, Foucault's essay 'What Is an Author?' is recklessly unhistorical.[22] Vickers also argues with Jeffrey Masten, whose book *Textual Intercourse* depicts collaborative authorship in the period as an alternative norm, homosocial and even homoerotic, whereas our modern view of authorship is seen as bedevilled by a patriarchal obsession with individual possession.[23] It is not inconceivable that both sides of the argument could be right. It is also possible that both sides are opposing the same problem, which is that a Bardolatrous attachment to Shakespeare might marginalize his collaborative works, and indeed obscure the fact of their collaborative nature. Vickers pursues this goal by defining and evaluating Shakespeare's contribution, McMullan and Masten by presenting collaborative works as viable, unified, and whole. When the cases are put like this, it does not take strenuous mental gymnastics to believe both. In this book the collaborative plays from the end of Shakespeare's career are treated as wholes, and it is assumed that joint authorship does not require a partial commitment to the overall project from each author. On the other hand, when the particulars of form and content are addressed it is illuminating to identify the probable individual author, in order to clarify the way in which a particular speech or scene relates to other late Shakespearian work.

So the assumptions in this study are: that collaborative plays are at the heart of the late Shakespearian canon; that they are in effect fully authorized by Shakespeare, even if only partly written by him; that the whole of a collaborative play is admissible evidence; that, nevertheless, those parts of the plays that are thought to be Shakespeare's might have special weight. It is necessary to assert the thematic qualities that bind the romances with the collaborative plays that followed them, in order to develop the notion that Shakespeare was indeed pursuing some distinctive and new aims in his late work. The value of *The Tempest* as the last solo-authored play does persist, however. It takes new angles on, and finds temporary conclusions to, a wide variety of key themes. Its central character takes unprecedented control of the play in which he serves, and then finds his creation eluding him. The suggestiveness of this as an analogy for Shakespeare and his career cannot wholly be set aside even once the continuation of Shakespeare's career, and its continued engagement with the interests of the romances, has been taken on board.

G. Wilson Knight's *The Crown of Life* (1946) stretches its canon to include *Henry VIII*, but it does so in order to define another climactic point in Shakespeare's career. Knight writes very differently from Derek Traversi about the finality of *The Tempest*, even though he praises Prospero as a 'myth of the national soul'. He is leaving room for another play: '*The Tempest* would scarcely have been quite satisfying as Shakespeare's last play, since despite its many subtle recapitulations, it might yet seem to dissolve the stern political and national interest of earlier works into a haze of esoteric mysticisms. One expects, from such a poet, a less visionary and enigmatic conclusion.'[24] In fact it is quite possible to argue there is a 'visionary and enigmatic conclusion' to *Henry VIII* as well. *The Crown of Life* was written mainly in summer 1944, and the presence of war is felt in the book's profound patriotism. Knight's terms ('stern political and national interest') are just as conditioned by their milieu as, perhaps, our own tendency to see greater scepticism. This is Knight on the final moments of the climactic play, *Henry VIII*, where Archbishop Cranmer prophesies about the infant Elizabeth. He predicts that Henry's daughter will be a glorious queen, which for a Jacobean audience was a past event. As will be seen below, it is a rather edgy speech, but for Knight it demonstrates a national characteristic without ambiguity:

Cranmer's words define not merely a single monarch's reign, but rather the Phoenix excellence, reminiscent of other Phoenix passages in Shakespeare, of an undying purity and blessedness settling here, on England. Though in contrast to our tragic mysticism this may seem a view of merely temporal felicity, yet the temporality is shot through with eternal meaning, and immortal. (p. 260)

For Knight the point is to pursue the definitive concluding moment. In this book, however, the value of expanding the canon will be to open up multiple, sometimes fragmentary, explorations of repeating artistic characteristics.

Robert M. Adams's otherwise interesting and useful book *Shakespeare: The Four Romances* works (as its title states) with a restricted 'late' canon. In an appendix he is acerbic about the claim of *Henry VIII*:

One sure thing is that *Henry VIII*, whoever wrote it and in whatever context we view it, has precious little to do with the romances. 'All is true' alone marks it as of another world, a world apart from Pentapolis, Sicilia, and that rarer island where Caliban still snuffles in the mud, snaring the nimble marmoset, and dreaming of something wonderful in the clouds that strains our imaginations to conceive. Mopsa, Dorcas, and their ilk will make up the audience to which the subtitle 'all is true' most naturally appeals.[25]

This is a drastic misreading of the play's alternative title *All Is True*, the obviousness of which hints at its own deception. The play is actually full of challenging ideas about, and ambivalent representations of, complex historical truth. In fact, at times it is sharply ironic, and is part of exactly what Adams denies—the representation of a world of imagination, that in this case bears a strong but out-of-phase resemblance to history. *Henry VIII* is a history play subtly affected by the dynamics of romance. The detail of this claim will be explored throughout this book, but it can be made in more structural terms with reference to the end of the play. Archbishop Cranmer prophesies a glorious future for the Princess Elizabeth:

> Let me speak, sir,
> For heaven now bids me, and the words I utter
> Let none think flattery, for they'll find 'em truth.
>
> (5.4.14–16)

Here the issue of truth is clearly under strain. The first audiences of this play had, no doubt, nostalgic affection for the dead Queen and would not necessarily rebel against this prophecy as mere flattery. However, this does not foreclose the question entirely. Cranmer appeals to a new authority in his words, which is corroborated but complicated by the fact that he is prophesying things that have already happened at the time of the play's performance. He praises the Queen that Elizabeth will become, venturing into biblical comparison: 'Saba [Sheba] was never | More covetous of wisdom and fair virtue | Than this pure soul shall be' (5.1.23–5).[26] As Cranmer approaches more recent history things get complicated, as praising the former Queen does not easily sit alongside praise of the current King. The prophecy blurs these things together, but much is unsaid:

> God shall be truly known, and those about her
> From her shall read the perfect ways of honour,
> And by those claim their greatness, not by blood.
> Nor shall this peace sleep with her, but, as when
> The bird of wonder dies—the maiden phoenix—
> Her ashes new create another heir
> As great in admiration as herself,
> So shall she leave her blessèdness to one,
> When heaven shall call her from this cloud of darkness,
> Who from the sacred ashes of her honour
> Shall star-like rise as great in fame as she was,
> And so stand fixed. Peace, plenty, love, truth, terror,
> That were the servants to this chosen infant,
> Shall then be his, and, like a vine, grow to him.
>
> (5.4.36–49)

There is an enormous amount at stake in this speech. Cranmer is skating over turbulent history. The reign of Elizabeth's half-sister, Mary I, in which Cranmer himself was executed for heresy, is alluded to in the idea that under the Protestant Queen 'God shall be truly known'. He also smoothes over the controversy and anxiety surrounding King James's succession. This is a piece of propaganda styled as prophecy, but the form does leave the reader able to see around its narrow terms. The clash of tenses—the 'were' in line 48 finds past, present, and future clashing together—helps induce an awareness of the problems behind the assertions. For now the important thing is that the version of history found in *Henry VIII* can be seen as part of Shakespeare's exploration of the boundaries of a rather surprising genre in this context: romance, and particularly the version developed in Shakespeare's recent plays, is a significant reference point for the spiritual tone of hope in these closing moments. As well as a heightened atmosphere at times, as in this scene of mystical prophecy, *Henry VIII* also shares with romance a structure with a strong providential style, a period of tribulation for its central figures, and (a particularly late Shakespearian feature) a strong presence for the family. It centres on dynastic trauma and the hope found in new generations, and it creates a supernatural atmosphere even as it tells a kind of verifiable truth. Much like Leontes, Pericles, Cymbeline, and Prospero, Henry finds redemption in his daughter.

It is easier to argue that the other extant Shakespeare–Fletcher collaboration, *The Two Noble Kinsmen*, is a continuation of the exploration of romance. Here Chaucer is the main source, and a conduit for a long tradition. The story is derived from Greek myths, via Statius's *Thebaid* and Boccaccio's *Decameron*, as well as *The Knight's Tale*. In contrast to these ancient roots, it has been argued that this play was written to make part of the celebrations of James I's daughter Elizabeth's marriage to Duke Frederick the Elector Palatine—and was performed there alongside other romances, some of which may have been revised for the occasion.[27] Thus it puts the medieval-classical story into a contemporary situation. Nevertheless, Robert Adams is even more scornful of *The Two Noble Kinsmen* than he is of *Henry VIII*. Again he chooses to take at face value something that is actually rather subtle. The tonal complexity of the play, as it switches between plangent emotion and near-farcical humour, is seen as plain travesty: 'Whatever parts of *The Two Noble Kinsmen* are assignable to Shakespeare, the flip-flop ending, in which Emilia is dealt off first to one noble knight and then to his Tweedledee alternative, comes close to reducing the entire story to a self-parody' (Adams, 175). As will be seen later in the book, the great pathos of the central relationship between Palamon and Arcite survives but is also compromised by an atmosphere that is ironic, even sceptical. In Helen Cooper's view, Shakespeare 'ends his career in the bleakness of a medieval romance that goes wrong'.[28] However, it may be that the tones and genres with which the play interacts are managed with great care, and held in a delicate but arresting balance. The evaluation of the story is not clearly resolved, and the audience is left to ponder a literary experiment. The Chaucerian source, then, is tested in the new literary environment, as is its version of romance. If it does become 'self-parody', then it does so for a purpose.

In a part of the play that is thought to be Shakespearian, Emilia prays to Diana as a protest against the tournament about to be fought over her. In addressing the goddess of chastity, she becomes part of a complex web of ideas relating to purity, marriage, and the entrance into maturity, that also surrounds the other heroines in the romances. This is her moment of resistance amid a traumatic transition:

> *Still music of recorders. Enter Emilia in white, her*
> *hair about her shoulders, with a wheaten wreath;*
> *one in white holding up her train, her hair stuck*
> *with flowers; one before her carrying a silver hind*
> *in which is conveyed incense and sweet odours,*
> *which being set upon the altar, her maids standing*
> *apart, she sets fire to it. Then they curtsy and kneel*

EMILIA (*praying to Diana*)
> O sacred, shadowy, cold, and constant queen,
> Abandoner of revels, mute contemplative,
> Sweet, solitary, white as chaste, and pure
> As wind-fanned snow, who to thy female knights
> Allow'st no more blood than will make a blush,
> Which is their order's robe: I here, thy priest,
> Am humbled fore thine altar. O, vouchsafe
> With that thy rare green eye, which never yet
> Beheld thing maculate, look on thy virgin;
> And, sacred silver mistress, lend thine ear—
> Which ne'er heard scurril term, into whose port
> Ne'er entered wanton sound—to my petition,
> Seasoned with holy fear. This is my last
> Of vestal office. I am bride-habited,
> But maiden-hearted. A husband I have 'pointed,
> But do not know him. Out of two, I should
> Choose one and pray for his success, but I
> Am guiltless of election.

(5.3.1–18)

The mysterious atmosphere of this scene is set out in a detailed stage direction—an unusual feature that this play shares with other late works. It might well be due to the technique of a scribe, Ralph

Crane, who incorporated his memories of performances.[29] It may be that, as Stephen Orgel argues in his notes to the storm scene in *The Tempest*, these directions are written for readers, and that the scribal presentation of Shakespeare's texts (and possibly the author's own, in his papers, though this cannot be shown) was newly oriented towards print consumption.[30] Alternatively, greater detail in staging and a great importance attached to this detail might explain it. Music is playing, as it often is at supernatural moments in late Shakespeare. The invocation of classical gods is typical, though the specifically classical setting is not always there to support it. Diana herself appears as *deus ex machina* in *Pericles*; in *The Two Noble Kinsmen* she does not exactly intervene, but then Emilia does not exactly ask her to do anything other than to let the best man win. Alongside the stillness and gravity there is the rhetorical intensity that can be seen elsewhere in the romances, particularly in scenes where a spiritual scale is approached. The language—'mute contemplative', 'maculate', 'scurrile', 'bride-habited'—is more ornate than usual. It works in the same way as Cranmer's prophecy, creating a heightened atmosphere very much in keeping with climactic moments in romance.

As the third possible Shakespeare–Fletcher collaboration (the lost play *Cardenio*) shows, the significance of these later works in the context of this book can just be a result of their being romance in any sense. The tight chronological group of the classic canon of four romances is not final, and is instead followed by a more dispersed and varied continuation of the exploration of the mode. Any discussion of *Cardenio* requires great care, but even the barest probable facts of its existence are suggestive. It does not appear in the Folio or any surviving contemporary Quarto. However, there are two records in the Lord Chamberlain's papers of a play called *Cardenno* or *Cardenna*, indicating one or two court performances in 1612–13. Then there is silence until 1653 when the publisher Humphrey Moseley announces in the register of the Stationers' Company his intention and right to publish what seems to be the same play. He calls it 'The History of Cardenio, by Mr Fletcher and Shakespeare'.[31] At this time the theatres were all closed during the Civil War, and the stock of the King's Men had passed to Moseley. He was opportunistically printing any obscurities found therein. However, as far as we can ascertain, he did not actually print *Cardenio*. Then there is further silence until 1728, when Lewis Theobald published and performed (to much acclaim) his play *Double Falshood*, which says on its title-page that it was 'written originally by William Shakespeare'. Theobald edited Shakespeare's works, so is in this way a respectable source for the claim, but he was also accused of plagiarism, which creates suspicion, and he did not include *Cardenio* in his edition.

Even its title suggests something, namely that it was based on the story of Cardenio (a tragicomic tale of betrayal between friends, thwarted love, disguise, and eventual resolution) in Cervantes's *Don Quixote*. Basing one of his final plays on this brilliant and sustained meditation on the nature of romance implies that Shakespeare had far from exhausted the mode by the time of *The Tempest*. As has been seen, the dialogue between romance and irony is fundamental to an understanding of late Shakespeare, and Cervantes certainly deployed profound irony in his own version. In *Don Quixote* the hero wills himself into a world of romance, and readers and characters can see the gaps between his fiction and reality. In fact, the work is a kind of counter-romance, exploding its fantastic elements. So any connection between Shakespearian romance and Cervantes is suggestive because it means that the English author was involved in a wider consideration of his current mode of writing. Of course Fletcher may have instigated the connection, and the fact that *Don Quixote* was then being translated by Shelton makes it an available source that Shakespeare might have mined for stories much as he did Italian novellas or chronicle histories—that is, without a strategic conceptual goal in mind.[32] So, although the status of *Cardenio* is fraught, it is still worth pursuing it, as the idea that Shakespeare thought about different varieties of romance is so important.

Jonathan Bate has made a convincing case that *Double Falshood* might indeed contain relics of a lost Shakespeare play.[33] He notes that in 1728 contemporary opinion went both ways, with the *Weekly Journal* concluding that Theobald revered Shakespeare too greatly to fake a play, while the *Gentleman's Magazine* accused him of forgery. Bate also cites the fulsome dedication to George II, whose special permission Theobald had obtained in order to have sole rights over the play. So if he is lying, he has taken a huge risk by associating the King. Of course, Theobald could simply be mistaken, but the earlier mentions of the name of the play make that unlikely. One curious aspect of Theobald's argument is that he says he had three manuscripts of the original, none of which survives (in itself not surprising)—but whether this adds to or detracts from credibility is a moot point.

Other pieces of evidence produced by Bate add strength to the possibility that *Double Falshood* is a relic of *Cardenio*. It is indeed based on the story of Cardenio in *Don Quixote*. Theobald did not know about earlier mentions of the lost play and its title, so it would be a remarkable coincidence for him to have used the same source. Close analysis suggests that the 1612 translation by Shelton (a likely prompt for the Shakespeare–Fletcher play in the first place) is the direct source, rather than any of the translations published between then and Theobald's own time. The language of *Double Falshood* does not seem to be uniformly Theobald's own—indeed, it seems most likely that the second half recalls Fletcher, while the first part recalls Shakespeare. It would be inconceivable for someone to forge a Shakespeare–Fletcher collaboration at this time because nobody thought that the two authors actually collaborated. *The Two Noble Kinsmen* was attributed to Fletcher or to Fletcher and Beaumont. *Henry VIII*, which appeared in the First Folio, was thought of as Shakespeare's alone. Indeed, Theobald's acknowledgement, in his preface, that detractors have identified the style of Fletcher in the play, now looks honest and uncanny. Also, Theobald in 1728 did not know about the record of a court performance of *Cardenio*, nor of Humphrey Moseley's assertion of the right to print it in 1653. These pieces of evidence seem to Bate, and to me, to add substance to the idea that there is a relic of an adapted *Cardenio* in this much later work. Theobald admits that the manuscripts date from after the Restoration, so may well have been adapted (as other plays were at that time) before he himself adapted them. Conclusions drawn from the play thus have questionable weight, but the facts of Shakespeare's interest in Cervantes and further exploration of romance are significant enough on their own.

A further necessary note of caution: when readers have encountered some lines in Act 1 Scene 3 they have often made a connection with Shakespeare. Henriquez is waiting for Violante below her window. Like a character in late Shakespeare he calls for music:

> Th' obscureness of her birth
> Cannot eclipse the lustre of her eyes,
> Which make her all one light. Strike up, my masters,
> But touch the strings with a religious softness.
> Teach sound to languish through the night's dull ear,
> 'Till melancholy start from her lazy couch,
> And carelessness grow convert to attention.[34]

The dreamy tone and the 'religious softness' create an atmosphere reminiscent of Shakespearian romance, though perhaps the apostrophe here is more mannered than we might expect, with its personified abstractions piled up. Nevertheless the Shakespearian note was marked and praised by the text's earliest readers, which prompted Theobald to claim emphatically that these were his lines and his alone. Of course they may be effective Shakespearian pastiche within a wider context of direct inheritance—but this is an instructive warning. However, at the beginning of 4.2 another musical moment does suggest further affinity with Shakespeare's late work along these lines:

> JULIO   Ha! Hark, a sound from heaven! Do you hear nothing?
> GENTLEMAN   Yes, sir: the touch of some sweet instrument.
>   There's no inhabitant.
> JULIO   No, no, the better.
> GENTLEMAN   This is a strange place to hear music in.
> JULIO   I'm often visited with some sweet airs.
>   The spirit of some hapless man that died,
>   And left his love hid in a faithless woman,
>   Sure haunts these mountains.
>
>   *Violante sings within.*
>
>   (4.2.8–15)

The music is real and explicable, but it is also heavenly and mysterious—as will be seen, such a double existence is seen elsewhere in Shakespeare's late work. At this point Julio, acting mad in the mountains, is Caliban-like in a variety of ways, and it is Caliban in Shakespeare who notes the 'sweet airs' of the island. However, this again seems like pastiche—but it could be Fletcher's pastiche as well as Theobald's. Throughout the play there are hints of Shakespeare, and especially late Shakespeare, but there is often this sense of secondariness, or pastiche. This does not mean that the work is faking a Shakespearian quality; we may even infer that Shakespeare himself was reflecting on his own recent creations. Most of all it acts as a persistent reminder that one should not get too exercised by the resemblance of *Double Falshood* to the other plays discussed in this book.

Cardenio will play only a small role in this study because there is not space for, nor much hope of, fully accounting for its features. Nevertheless there is a good chance that Shakespeare, along with Fletcher, pursued romance further in an adaptation of a story from *Don Quixote*, in which they revisited moments from other romances and may even have pastiched famous features of those plays. The play's uses of disguise, mistaken identity, and tragicomic love stories are much like those of the other romances. The answer to the question that initiated this exploration must be that the end-point of late Shakespeare is indeed the very end of Shakespeare's career, and that the questions posed and faced by the three or four romances of the classic canon are also being posed and faced in the collaborative plays that immediately follow them. Chapter 6 will take on the two most important collaborative relationships (with Fletcher and Middleton) directly, in order to outline their very different characteristics. This also adds to the book a sense of how the next generation inherited Shakespeare's work and moved on from it, a process already in evidence at times in the late collaborations.

The *terminus* of the late work is marked by the end of Shakespeare's literary output, wherever that line is drawn, but the beginning lacks such a definite point. In Chapter 3 I shall make a case for seeing a number of inaugural qualities in *Pericles*, which incorporates ideas of new discovery and changing direction within its plot and characters. Critics have extrapolated from this to a biographical reading: *Pericles* has been seen as a restoration of faith in people, and in art, that results from Shakespeare emerging from a period of despair. In such an account, the works that belong to this dark period are *Timon of Athens* and especially *Coriolanus*, the closest in time to the romances.[35] The former is an important part of Shakespeare's literary relationship with Thomas Middleton (the probable co-author), and as such will be featured briefly in Chapter 6. Despite these degrees of proximity there are clear differences in genre and tone between these two bleak and bitter tragedies and the romances. So there is a possible dividing line, but from this point on, the issue gets more complicated.

This book will explore aspects of Shakespeare's late work that separate it from the rest of his career. However, it will also include discussion of features of earlier works that are revisited and reworked in the late plays, in order to reconnect them with their origins, and to demonstrate that the 'late' features are not exclusively so. *Antony and Cleopatra*, for example, features an interplay of spectacle, wonder, and sceptical reason that has much in common with extravagant displays in *The Winter's Tale*, *The Tempest*, and elsewhere. This will be discussed in detail in Chapter 2. In this case there is temporal proximity—*Antony and Cleopatra* was most likely written in 1606. In the case of *The Two Gentlemen of Verona*, which is featured in Chapter 7, the time-gap is much larger, yet there are various kinds of continuity between the earliest and the latest works. There is not room here to discuss many of them. Elsewhere, however, I have explored a thread connecting *The Comedy of Errors*, *Twelfth Night*, and *The Tempest*.[36] These are the three plays which stick closest to the neoclassical principles of dramatic decorum, wherein the time and space of the action are limited. Any number of other thematic continuities could have been identified. The ones chosen for Chapter 7 illuminate a particular tendency in Shakespeare's late rethinkings: when he reworks the intensity of jealousy found in *Othello* in *The Winter's Tale*, he gives the romance audience a different perspective, from outside the maelstrom of emotion. So there is an interesting tension in any attempt to demarcate the late work, between the need to register its evident differences, and the need to consider the repeated features. This is a necessary qualification of this book's central belief (retained nevertheless) that Shakespeare's late work does exist as a discernible category.

There is one further way in which the search for a beginning to late Shakespeare is complicated. Until the late twentieth century, the traditional image of Shakespeare as an author tended to be of a spontaneous genius who wrote plays once and then moved on. The survival of significantly different versions of some plays (*King Lear* and *Hamlet* in particular) was usually explained by the agency of someone other than the author, garbling or cutting the text in response to contingencies that had no bearing on the essential nature of the play. From the 1980s onward it gradually became more widely accepted that these variant texts might result from a process of authorial revision.

Thus a new and, to my mind, more plausible and impressive image of Shakespeare emerges: that of an author engaged in the theatrical process, amending plays as they are performed and reperformed, regularly revising. A curious piece of evidence from the period gives a flavour of playgoing: Simon Forman, an astrologer and quack doctor with courtly contacts, kept records of miscellaneous activities which survive today. It includes descriptions of four plays he saw in 1611: these include the recent *Cymbeline* and *Winter's Tale*, but also the five-year old *Macbeth*.[37] It was, unsurprisingly, common practice to include old plays in any theatrical season, and it seems highly probable that these would be adapted to a greater or lesser extent, in the light of new circumstances, previous experience, or even because of renewed creative input. The key example is *King Lear*, of which the first Quarto (Q1) was published in 1608. There was a second Quarto (Q2) in 1619. The First Folio of Shakespeare's works, put together from generally very authoritative manuscripts by Heminge and Condell, was published in 1623. In general, and specifically in this case, the texts of the First Folio tend to have fewer obvious errors. Q2 is full of interest for considering fine details, but the real dynamic is between Q1 and F, texts which contain large differences. It is most likely that the later, Folio text of *King Lear* represents Shakespeare's own alterations to the earlier version as represented by the Quarto text. In the Oxford Shakespeare, in contrast with preceding collected editions, there are two texts of *King Lear*, based on Q1 and F, and named accordingly *The History of King Lear* (as is Q1), and *The Tragedy of King Lear* (as is F). The Folio revision is dated *c.*1610, which makes the Folio *Lear*, in effect, late Shakespeare.[38]

Before considering the ramifications of this particular text and its contribution to the canon of Shakespeare's late work, it is worth briefly broadening the implications of revision. It may be that the plays on which scholars of revision focus are anomalous not because they have been revised, but because the evidence of revision has survived. There is every reason to imagine that many other Shakespeare plays were performed in differing versions, but when we only have one text to work with this cannot be seen. The case of *Macbeth* is extreme but instructive: as will be explored in Chapter 6, the single extant text (from the First Folio of 1623) may well date from after Shakespeare's retirement, even after his death, and was put together well after the play was first written. So Shakespeare's late work might include not just those plays first written after 1608 or so, but also those rewritten during that period. When plays were revived for new performances Shakespeare, as a stakeholder in the theatre company, had access to the manuscripts. These may have been updated for a whole variety of reasons. After a substantial gap of time changing taste may have obliged some amendments; over a shorter timescale it would have been easy to remember which parts of the play worked well in performance, and which did not. Either way, the conditions for revision were there. Such an approach is liable to a great deal of speculation: in practice it is only the Folio *King Lear* that offers both the text and the context to connect it with the late plays. The revisions in question create a distinctly different play, one that is more streamlined and focused than its Quarto predecessor, and one that does seem to have been rewritten in line with, and in reaction to, the prevailing mode and style of Shakespeare's late work.

John Jones's book *Shakespeare at Work* gives a vivid account of the process of revision in *King Lear*, *Hamlet*, and *Othello*. Jones is receptive to the fine detail of revision (odd words inserted or changed here and there) as well as to the larger sections that come into and out of the text, and he is bold enough to assert the deliberate process behind the changes he considers.[39] Jones has a counterintuitive theory of the purposes behind the revision of *Lear* that links it closely to the late works written at the same time as the Folio text. Jones sees the Quarto text as a sharp-edged mixture of genres which includes speeches and scenes that anticipate the late romances. In the Folio revision, Jones argues, Shakespeare was able to see where these had led, having started work on romance itself. Hence he clarified the genre and nature of *King Lear*. Two examples of the phenomenon Jones describes show the value of this argument. In the scene where the returned Cordelia witnesses attempts to cure her father (4.7) the Folio version (lines 24–5) omits a call for music that in Quarto accompanies the King's revival. Hermione's staged resurrection in *The Winter's Tale* is one of several late Shakespearian scenes that integrate the music into the other-worldly atmosphere of romance. For Jones, the revising Shakespeare recognized the anticipatory quality of the musical revival in Quarto *King Lear*, and he removed it.[40] In a scene which is completely omitted from the Folio, describing events in the

French camp, Jones notes the presence of a lingering description of Cordelia:

GENTLEMAN   Ay, sir. She took them, read them in my presence,
And now and then an ample tear trilled down
Her delicate cheek. It seemed she was a queen
Over her passion who, most rebel-like,
Sought to be king o'er her.
KENT   O, then it moved her.
GENTLEMAN   Not to a rage. Patience and sorrow strove
Who should express her goodliest. You have seen
Sunshine and rain at once; her smiles and tears
Were like, a better way. Those happy smilets
That played on her ripe lip seemed not to know
What guests were in her eyes, which parted thence
As pearls from diamonds dropped. In brief,
Sorrow would be a rarity most beloved
If all could so become it.

                 (*The History of King Lear*, Scene 17, 12–25)

The Winter's Tale offers an interesting comparison for this description of conflicting emotions held in perfect balance: the mixed feelings of Paulina as described by the Gentlemen of 5.2 (lines 72–5). More generally, the late plays' paragon-daughters, who are also discussed in awestruck tones, are analogues for Cordelia. For Jones, the omission of such a scene from F results from Shakespeare clarifying the genre and even periodization of his own career. This is a bold and fascinating conclusion, not stopping at the image of Shakespeare-the-reviser, but positing an even more self-conscious author who thought about the organization of his works into genres and periods. This is rather different from the natural genius, or the writer always responding to theatrical contingencies.

    The revision of the Folio *Lear* has a sting in its tail, however, that suggests that the process of generic refinement and definition could not fully stifle the emerging dramatic possibilities of Shakespeare's late work. *King Lear* occupies an interesting position both before and after *Pericles*—it provides a model for that play's abject King, and then itself has *Pericles* as a model. So the differences in tone at the moment of Lear's death might reflect the state of the play before and after Shakespearian romance not just in time, but also in mood. It leads towards a counterweight to Jones's conclusion, because here it seems as if the possibilities of romance make a sharp difference to the closing moments of the Folio *Lear*:

> LEAR   And my poor fool is hanged. No, no, no life?
> Why should a dog, a horse, a rat have life,
> And thou no breath at all? Thou'lt come no more.
> Never, never, never, never, never.
> [*To Kent*] Pray you, undo this button. Thank you, sir.
> Do you see this? Look on her. Look, her lips.
> Look there, look there.   *He dies.*
>
>   (5.3.281–7)

The two lines at the end of this speech are not in Q1. For A. C. Bradley they indicate that the old King dies in a state of 'unbearable joy', seeing his daughter alive, but it is debatable how much the audience shares or experiences this consolation.[41] He could, for example, be witnessing the soul leaving the body, or telling himself the last in a line of lies. None the less, if Bradley's reading is at all viable, Shakespeare allows the possibility of an astonishing moment of hope just at the point of the play where it seems that nothing can be redeemed (a mood from which Q1 offers no release). This is a kind of false recognition, whereas in the romances the recognitions are true (and they are recognitions of truth itself). It may serve to emphasize the unmitigated nature of Lear's loss, as his feeble gesture at belief in something better is hollow in the context of this brutal play. Nevertheless Lear's tragic recognition (of his own culpability) is followed by a feint towards a comic or romantic recognition, and this makes a great difference to these final moments. The Folio's added lines, then, have a double interaction with late Shakespearian motifs that deepens and complicates any idea of the Folio *Lear* as a 'late work'. It recalls moments where characters come back to life, or seem to do so, in *Pericles*, *Cymbeline*, *The Winter's Tale*, and (less explicitly) in *The Tempest*. The revival of Cordelia works in a parallel way, though its effect is suitably tuned to, and untuned by, the tragic context. The revision of *King Lear* exemplifies the fact that the creative process of Shakespeare's career was not limited to the writing of single works on single occasions. It also included, most likely, regular revising and updating of works for new performances. The second conclusion one might draw from the Folio *Lear* is even more significant: it suggests that Shakespeare thought of his career in

a way not entirely unlike modern critics, and that this book's attempt
to anatomize a phase of his work actually has something in common
with the way the author developed that phase.

Another facet of the late Shakespearian canon needs a brief mention.
The book *Shakespeares Sonnets* was published in 1609, and is thus a
contemporary of *Cymbeline* and *The Winter's Tale*. The latest ideas
about the composition of these poems suggest that it occurred in
phases. Two key periods were the early–mid 1590s (the heyday of
Elizabethan sonnets) and around 1600.[42] The question of how much
revision the sonnets underwent before they were first actually printed
is harder to resolve. Scholars have argued that the first sixty sonnets
may well have been reworked for the 1609 publication. This does
not necessitate, but it does not preclude, entirely new sonnets being
written to appear in the sequence. Many ideas that are crucial in
the romances—paternity, jealousy, time—are explored here too. In
the broadest sense the sonnets, then, could be considered as 'late
Shakespeare', and they offer a further indication that one should not
demarcate the boundaries of that canon too strictly.

From the revisions of *King Lear* there arise complex indications of
Shakespeare's awareness of categories within his work. From the
collaborations with Fletcher comes the sense that Shakespeare held a
persistent interest in the modes and genres of his writing, and took
opportunities to explore further. Thus it may be possible to discern
the integrity of a 'late' canon with a unified generic purpose. On
the other hand, the presence of revisions and collaborations with
their divergent characteristics, and the difficulty of demonstrating
anything like a clean break with earlier works, tend against such a
clean-cut topic for this book. It is necessary to proceed, then, with
a balanced awareness of what can, and what cannot, be asserted
about the distinctive characteristics of the late works and (much
more tentatively) about their suitability as artistic valedictions. The
broadened canon, in comparison with other attempts to establish the
nature of late Shakespeare, makes the argument less straightforward,
but potentially more compelling.

Seeing is Believing

When considering romance in general, it is not always a good idea to start at the end. Extended adventures, digressions, and encounters are vital: it is often better to focus on the process than on the goal. However, in Shakespearian romance—perhaps in dramatic romance overall—endings have special importance. The unfolding of time is a rich feature of the theatrical experience, and the ingenuity expended in testing the endurance of characters and audience never escapes the need for time to reveal all. In another sense, as has already been established, one should not be too end-obsessed in dealing with Shakespearian romance. However in this chapter *The Tempest*, that perennial pseudo-finale, is indeed the culmination of a key theme, and a new direction too. *The Winter's Tale* and *Cymbeline*, as well as *Antony and Cleopatra*, will feature most prominently, but much of what is said here is applicable to *Pericles*, *Henry VIII*, and *The Two Noble Kinsmen*. These plays also have an interplay between reason and spectacle; there too wondrous things are revealed to the sight of the audience, things that raise awkward questions. They also explore problems in the nature of truth, dramatic and otherwise.

Shakespeare's endings in comedy and romance are very often wonderful and desirable, but can prove improbable and even unsatisfying. Most readers of *As You Like It*, an earlier play, find that the discordant elements are overcome by the happiness of central characters and the play's resourcefulness in giving the audience an outlet for its cynicism. Rosalind is so worthy of happiness that her happiness has worth; Jaques is so fitted to melancholy that his exclusion suits him, and us, well. In *Measure for Measure* the discord overcomes everything else, taking its clearest form in the silence of Isabella when the Duke makes his timely but surprising offer of marriage. In the late romances Shakespeare seems to invite audiences and readers to face up to the dilemma in a way that is both more and less structured. Should one participate in joy and wonder, or should one remain crabbily on the edge? Should we remember all the deceit, subterfuge, and coincidence required to arrange what should be a natural ending, or should we accept, and learn from, the reward of virtue? The choice is more structured than that of comedy because it is schematic—the two sides exist in simultaneous contrast. It is also less structured, in that the plays do not offer decisive guidance or arbitration.

The metaphorical viewpoint of the audience is at issue, and this aspect of the plays is closely related to their testing of the audience's literal viewpoint. The question of how we 'see' a play as a set of moral questions is entwined with the question of how we see the play as a visual spectacle. This is partly a question of whose viewpoint we share on a given scene: often in drama the different eyes on stage will apprehend the play from alternative perspectives. At times the cynic's eye colours the action, at others that of the awestruck innocent. It is also a question of how the truth of representation works in the play. The numerous spectacular scenes test what may be performed plausibly, and the audience faces a deep and complex version of what Coleridge called the 'willing suspension of disbelief'.[1] In the romances the act of will comes to the surface, belief and disbelief are conscious processes, and any suspension is a decision to accept some or all aspects of the play. The action and words inspire wonder, but they oblige awkward thoughts about the truth of that wonder: the coexistence of these two things is vital.

In *Cymbeline* Giacomo the devious Italian affects the visual presentation of Innogen's bedroom in the process of winning a bet with Posthumus—having conned his way in, he will gather the evidence that will convince her husband of infidelity. His eyes drink in the setting, but we see complex effects as the room is changed by his viewpoint, and then his viewpoint is complicated by literary precedents:

> The crickets sing, and man's o'er-laboured sense
> Repairs itself by rest. Our Tarquin thus
> Did softly press the rushes ere he wakened

The chastity he wounded.
...
                    No more. To what end?
Why should I write this down that's riveted,
Screwed to my memory? She hath been reading late,
The tale of Tereus. Here the leaf's turned down
Where Philomel gave up.

                    (2.2.11–14, 42–6)

The whole scene is awkward to watch, because we are conscious that our own presence in this room replicates and compounds Giacomo's deed. The things he sees are displayed to general view and the corrupting influence affects them too. The scene is strengthened by the presence of stories—here the myths of two victims of rape, Lucrece and Philomel—which provide dark parallels to the action. The wager plot is comic by nature, but here we see a slippage of genre. Giacomo changes the usual emphasis in the stories he mentions. By saying 'our Tarquin', he recognizes that he and the Roman King share Italian origins; by calling it 'the tale of Tereus', he shifts the emphasis away from its heroine; by saying Philomel 'gave up', he misrepresents the violent struggle of her rape. The tale of Philomel from Ovid's *Metamorphoses* here makes a remarkable second appearance on Shakespeare's stage both as underlying theme and as a physical book; the other is in *Titus Andronicus* 4.1. In the *Cymbeline* scene, then, the audience is conscious of eyes being altered, viewpoints changing, and reality shifting.

Giacomo describes the details of the room, some of which might well have been unstaged in the Jacobean theatre. This puts further pressure on the relationship between dramatic reality and what we see. Many of the visual treats of Shakespeare's theatre are actually conjured in language, but words can come from sources of dubious veracity. It is not that we think that Giacomo is inventing the decor of her room when he describes it to Posthumus—he agrees with the description—but that there is an uncomfortable feeling that its lack of objective existence means it becomes a token within a nasty, misogynistic male bet. One story told to Posthumus strikes a chord within Shakespeare's work:

                    First, her bedchamber—
Where I confess I slept not, but profess

Had that was well worth watching—it was hanged
With tapestry of silk and silver; the story
Proud Cleopatra when she met her Roman,
And Cydnus swelled above the banks, or for
The press of boats or pride: a piece of work
So bravely done, so rich, that it did strive
In workmanship and value; which I wondered
Could be so rarely and exactly wrought,
Such the true life on't was.

(2.4.66–76)

Posthumus interrupts and seeks more esoteric information, which Giacomo is happy to deliver. That Giacomo should connect this famous scene of seduction and display from Plutarch's *Life of Antony* with Innogen's sleeping body reveals his misreading of her actions: she is innocent yet to him she is coquettish. When Cleopatra is imagined meeting 'her' Roman the possessive adjective could imply that at the same moment Innogen is meeting, and seducing, *her* Roman, Giacomo. In this scene, then, the audience sees things that are not actually there in a variety of ways, and the fact that it is as plain as the nose on your face that Innogen is blameless does not mean that it can be seen. Viewpoints in drama shift and swerve, led in uncomfortable directions by the distorted eyes of those onstage.

The interactions of this description are yet more complex, because the scene is not only well known from Plutarch, but also from Shakespeare's own play *Antony and Cleopatra* (2.2.197–233). There it is the gruff observer Enobarbus who offers an uncharacteristic, rapt account of the queen's arrival. The scene being retold is a dramatic one—perhaps we could expect Shakespeare's audience to remember a play first seen only a few years before (and quite possibly performed more recently). It is also a natural connection for modern readers who know their Shakespeare to make. This makes the dazzling but perhaps truncated reference to 'the true life on't' all the more sharp. This is usually glossed as a description of the picture's realism: it is true to life. However, it also hints at the 'true life' that preceded the representation, the event itself. Then there are two possibilities, both strange and rich, both expanding the dimensions of this scene in a way that adds further to the feeling that Innogen's story is being woven around her in a way over which she has no control. One is that Giacomo was actually there, or had spoken to someone who was actually there, when Cleopatra arrived on her barge. The two plays, though very different, inhabit the same historical time-frame. Though the Rome visited by Posthumus seems quite modern, the Romans who visit Britain are classical, and specifically locatable, as is Cymbeline himself, in the years shortly after the death of Cleopatra. The other possibility is that Giacomo's presence at the Cydnus scene was at a dramatic performance, and that this is an actor recalling something experienced as an actor. (There is a parallel in *Hamlet*, where there are hints that the actors playing Hamlet and Polonius may previously have played the roles of Brutus and Caesar in *Julius Caesar*.[2]) Either way, we can say at least that the notion of 'true life' has become considerably more complicated.

Antony and Cleopatra is a precedent to the romances in its complex interactions of seeing and believing. Shakespeare, with his constant interest in the nature of dramatic representation, includes versions of this dynamic throughout his career, but the profusion and centrality of the issue is greater in later works. *Antony and Cleopatra* is usually dated to 1606 or 1607, which puts it shortly before *Pericles*, and shortly before the cynical despair of *Coriolanus* and perhaps *Timon*, depending on its date. It has things in common with both. On the one hand, its stark and unresolvable structure, with Rome and Egypt, Caesar and Antony, opposing poles that cannot meet except in conflict, connects with the last tragedies. On the other, the love-story of the play offers moments which, though not closely akin to romance in the generic sense, do offer the spectacle and wonder that the late plays also feature. In Cleopatra's final scene both these moods come together, and in doing so they offer audiences and readers a schematic yet unresolved dilemma in how to interpret the play. The scene is very carefully set. On the one side, the side of Egypt, there are two great lovers, the love and loyalty of servants, and extravagant beauty in language and in what the language describes. But there are also capriciousness, human weaknesses such as jealousy and greed, a lack of realism, and a fundamental changeability. On the Roman side there are realism and constancy taken to extremes in a political ideology represented by Octavius Caesar, which prizes decorum over individual expression. Under this code heightened experience is interpreted in terms of cold facts. The Roman side cannot ascend as high as the Egyptian world in language or aspiration, but it cannot descend so far into indignity and compromise. Those caught in the middle (Antony, Enobarbus) are torn apart.

This could make the play sound like a lofty dramatization of profound human truths, and that is a way of reading it. However, these two worlds operate also as two kinds of eyes through which to view the drama, both valid throughout, though dominant in turns. At the end they are in a fine balance, as will be seen. Apprehending this balance might lead to a heightened sense of choice, but the audience, as in the romances, does not have to jump one way or the other. The play can work just as powerfully if it creates a rich sense of multiple potential. The two suicides of the central characters both invite a dual response, either cynical or awestruck. Antony dies farcically, failing to kill himself efficiently and struggling under the false belief that Cleopatra is already dead. Nevertheless his commitment to the principle of love remains, and there is something impressive about his persistence in the face of adversity. This is especially so because for Antony it does not come easily; he changes his mind all the time. It takes a huge effort to adhere to his doomed, deluded plans.

The lovers make passionate claims for their greatness, but there is a lack of external corroboration. For every piece of praise from an Egyptian voice, there is a plainer Roman conclusion. On the level of logic or moral judgement one could opt for this side or that, but there is no underlying truth in the play behind either. The pressure from the poetry, however, has a strong counter-rational tendency. Selfish, inconsistent, calculating Cleopatra may be, but her end and its language invite wonder:

> CLEOPATRA Give me my robe. Put on my crown. I have
> Immortal longings in me. Now no more
> The juice of Egypt's grape shall moist this lip.
> *Charmian and Iras help her to dress*
> Yare, yare, good Iras, quick—methinks I hear
> Antony call. I see him rouse himself
> To praise my noble act. I hear him mock
> The luck of Caesar, which the gods give men
> To excuse their after wrath. Husband, I come.
> Now to that name my courage prove my title.
> I am fire and air; my other elements
> I give to baser life. So, have you done?

Come then, and take the last warmth of my lips.
> *She kisses them*

Farewell, kind Charmian. Iras, long farewell.
> *Iras falls and dies*

Have I the aspic in my lips? Dost fall?
If thou and nature can so gently part,
The stroke of death is as a lover's pinch,
Which hurts and is desired. Dost thou lie still?
If thus thou vanishest, thou tell'st the world
It is not worth leave-taking.

CHARMIAN   Dissolve, thick cloud, and rain, that I may say
The gods themselves do weep.

(5.2.275–95)

The poetry may be inflationary in two senses: it makes the moment bigger than itself, but could also devalue it by altering the balance between poetry and substance. Cleopatra's eyes are fixed on another world altogether. Her body is fixed in its queenliness as she puts on her crown and robe, but also transcended, as she becomes, in words at least, 'fire and air'. Charmian's eyes are also important: she watches closely and reverently, and is convinced. Iras's participation in the scene is unspoken but absolute. She precedes her mistress into death. They are both lined up with the passion of the rhetoric. The scene continues in a similar vein:

CLEOPATRA   Peace, peace.
Dost thou not see my baby at my breast,
That sucks the nurse asleep?

CHARMIAN   O, break! O, break!

CLEOPATRA   As sweet as balm, as soft as air, as gentle.
O Antony!
> *She puts another aspic to her arm.*

Nay, I will take thee too.
What should I stay—   *She dies*

CHARMIAN   In this vile world? So, fare thee well.
Now boast thee, death, in thy possession lies
A lass unparalleled. Downy windows, close,
And golden Phoebus never be beheld
Of eyes again so royal! Your crown's awry.
I'll mend it, and then play—

(5.2.303–13)

308: vile] *Steevens*; wilde F1.
312: awry] *Rowe*; away F1.

Having seen death as a lover, she now sees the asp as her child, a troubling image which could be interpreted in rather sharp unmaternal Lady Macbeth-like ways—but it also offers a challenging beauty. Again Charmian's presence provides a strong image of how to receive the scene. For her this is a great and transcendent death, so she completes her mistress's line with conviction, imagining that she would have ended with a final gesture of superiority over the world. The change of the Folio (where it says 'wilde') text to 'vile' in modern editions is understandable and was first suggested in the eighteenth century by Steevens. There is nothing self-evidently wrong with 'wild[e]', though, and it retains the note of scorn while also imagining a more dynamically hostile world. The change of 'away' to 'awry', again an eighteenth-century innovation accepted by modern editors, is likewise sensible but also unnecessary. Indeed, 'away' rhymes with play, which creates a timely wistful note, and it can still suggest the right kind of displacement.[3]

Cleopatra's death is surrounded, then, by rhetorical and emotional pressure towards an awestruck interpretation. It needs it, because it is difficult to feel that Cleopatra in the play has earned her moment of plausible 'immortal longings', given her earthbound activities. (These great lovers have a delicately poised reputation through history: they are associated with passion and disaster, with excess in everything as the keynote.) It also needs it because the play ends with very different eyes upon the scene:

FIRST GUARD   This is an aspic's trail,
     And these fig-leaves have slime upon them such
     As th'aspic leaves upon the caves of Nile.
CAESAR   Most probable
     That so she died; for her physician tells me
     She hath pursued conclusions infinite
     Of easy ways to die. Take up her bed,
     And bear her women from the monument.
     She shall be buried by her Antony.
     No grave upon the earth shall clip in it
     A pair so famous. High events as these
     Strike those that make them, and their story is

No less in pity than his glory which
Brought them to be lamented. Our army shall
In solemn show attend this funeral,
And then to Rome. Come, Dolabella, see
High order in this great solemnity.

(5.2.344–60)

Caesar starts with a note of calculation, as he reveals the information
that the asp is not chosen for its symbolic suggestiveness, but simply
because it is an easy way to die. This neatly depicts the feet of clay
which hamper Cleopatra's transcendence. However, Caesar goes on
to praise this 'pair so famous', attributing to them a kind of greatness,
but one with a ring of empty celebrity rather than the achievements
he truly values. This is undercut by the chilling point that any pity
gravitating towards Antony and Cleopatra will be matched by the
glory heading for Caesar. The final analysis offers a new retrospective
reading of the suicide: it is merely a histrionic subtext to a political
triumph over a pair of deluded failures. Caesar is right, logically and
historically, but drama does not necessarily obey logic or history.
Caesar's words cannot wholly compromise the attraction of a wonder-
filled response. For the audience the two views exist together, both
viable, both problematic, and participate in the rich complexity of the
play.

The end of *Antony and Cleopatra* has a pattern shared by the
end of *The Winter's Tale*. Here again is a scene where the prosaic
view is available, but so are transcendence and wonder. Hermione's
transformation from a statue is a kind of reversal of the suicide of
Cleopatra. In the earlier play, a Queen creates a statue-like image of
herself as she enters death; in *The Winter's Tale* the Queen leaves the
statue state and returns to life. In neither case is the transformation
into or out of statue form a literal one, but the force of poetry and the
eyes of onstage beholders are able to create a kind of metamorphosis.
Hermione's transformation is a complete addition to Shakespeare's
source, Robert Greene's *Pandosto*. In Greene the Hermione figure
remains dead. It is a scene not out of place in romance, where marvels
and improbable secrecies often happen. Shakespeare prepares the
ground for the 'revival' with a view to more than one interpretation.
He makes sure that the rational explanation of Hermione's survival is
available, though itself far-fetched. There is considerable irony in the

last scene, as Leontes fails to pick up a number of clues that this is not actually a statue. First, Paulina has to explain away the ageing process:

> So much the more our carver's excellence,
> Which lets go by some sixteen years, and makes her
> As she lived now.
>
> (5.3.30–2)

Then she has to find a reason why Leontes must not touch the statue. Unlike Pygmalion, in the story from Ovid's *Metamorphoses* which is one precedent for the living-statue plot, Leontes will not feel the change happening as he kisses and caresses the model:

> Good my lord, forbear.
> The ruddiness upon her lip is wet.
> You'll mar it if you kiss it, stain your own
> With oily painting. Shall I draw the curtain?
>
> (5.3.80–3)

In retrospect the transformation is unmagical and these hints keep that in view throughout. However, other perspectives in the play cannot share the irony and our attention on these can operate as a way past doubt and towards some of the strangeness. For them the death of Hermione is no less real than that of her son Mamillius or of Antigonus. The latter actually sees the Queen's ghost in a dream; as he reports this there is no sense that he is wrong to assume that he is seeing an image of a dead person. The question of whether seeing is believing also for us is one that the play makes it difficult to answer. One key element of the question is found in Paulina's entreaty that her onstage audience should accept what they are seeing:

PAULINA   It is required
> You do awake your faith. Then, all stand still.
> Or those that think it is unlawful business
> I am about, let them depart.
LEONTES   Proceed.
> No foot shall stir.
PAULINA   Music; awake her; strike!
>   *Music*
> (*To Hermione*) 'Tis time. Descend. Be stone no more. Approach.
> Strike all that look upon with marvel. Come,

I'll fill your grave up. Stir. Nay, come away.
Bequeath to death your numbness, for from him
Dear life redeems you. (*To Leontes*) You perceive she stirs.

(5.3.94–103)

And finally we do perceive that she stirs, although it is more likely
that it has been an irresistible temptation throughout the scene to
stare at the actress playing Hermione and to watch for a flicker
or fidget. This is actually a significant part of the scene, as the
audience's lack of belief that Hermione is a statue about to come
to life is in curious harmony with an awareness that no actor can
truly become a statue. Paulina asks not only for 'faith' but also that
any who suspect her motive should leave; Leontes reassures her. The
audience is being faced with the option of a self-consciously open-
minded and wide-eyed reception of the scene. In the preceding scene
the reunion of Leontes and his lost daughter Perdita is not shown,
but is instead narrated by three detached and amused gentlemen.
One explanation for this is that underplaying the first reunion scene
allows the greater climax to emerge—replacing the muted ending
of Greene's *Pandosto* with something new and wonderful. We are
starved of seeing the first reunion, which heightens attention on
the second. Paulina and Leontes wave away doubters, and Paulina
describes what is about to occur as a resurrection, which it is, from
various viewpoints.

The negotiation between different ways of receiving this scene
is one carried out within the text. Here it is possibly useful to
think of Paulina as a theatrical figure, presenting the action for
an audience. Like Shakespeare, she offers the idea that this event
is improbable—'like an old tale'—but something 'appears' to be
happening: seeing is believing, she seems to argue. When Hermione
first speaks, her tone is not easily accommodated within a cynical
response to the scene:

PAULINA   That she is living,
Were it but told you, should be hooted at
Like an old tale. But it appears she lives,
Though yet she speak not. Mark a little while.
(*To Perdita*) Please you to interpose, fair madam. Kneel,
And pray your mother's blessing.—Turn, good lady,
Our Perdita is found.

HERMIONE   You gods, look down,
   And from your sacred vials pour your graces
   Upon my daughter's head.—Tell me, mine own,
   Where hast thou been preserved? Where lived? How found
   Thy father's court? For thou shalt hear that I,
   Knowing by Paulina that the oracle
   Gave hope thou wast in being, have preserved
   Myself to see the issue.
PAULINA   There's time enough for that,
   Lest they desire upon this push to trouble
   Your joys with like relation.

(5.3.116–31)

She invokes the gods and asks for blessings to be poured down onto her daughter. She also asks questions like someone who really has returned from a death-like absence. One dramatic precedent for this scene—it is probably not quite accurate to call it a source—is Euripides' Greek tragedy *Alcestis*. In this story, which also bears some resemblance to *Much Ado About Nothing,* Alcestis is rescued from the clutches of Death by Heracles and restored to her husband Admetus. There are other similarities: Admetus is forced to accept a veiled new wife before he knows it is really his old wife. This is very like *Much Ado,* but in *The Winter's Tale* too Leontes authorizes Paulina to make his marital decisions for him. The most telling thing here is that in this cognate story the heroine occupies a position between life and death. So Hermione's predecessor in this case comes closer to death than she does, but may contribute a deathly note in this scene. The things Hermione does not say are also revealing: by not speaking to Leontes she appears as someone changed, whose reintegration into the world will take time. And yet Hermione also makes explicit reference to the fact that she has been 'preserved' alive, neither dead nor a statue. She is not pretending to have been a statue, and yet she is acting like someone who has been transformed. Shakespeare manages to keep contradictory elements in the scene at the same time. Paulina's interruption is multifaceted: it is an act of sympathy, preserving Hermione from an outpouring of news, but it also protects Paulina and her plan, saving the moment of wonder without overexposing her subterfuge. In addition, it truncates the action in such a way as to enable multiple readings of the scene.

It reminds us of what must not be said, and keeps the revival enigmatic.

Hermione remains silent for the rest of the play, giving the audience no more clues to unpack her story. Leontes ends the play itself twenty lines later:

> Good Paulina,
> Lead us from hence, where we may leisurely
> Each one demand and answer to his part
> Performed in this wide gap of time since first
> We were disseverd. Hastily lead away.
>
> (5.3.152–6)

'Hastily' indeed: the scene of happy conclusions is a brittle one. Paulina's sudden marriage, Hermione's lack of words for her husband, the death of Mamillius, are discordant elements of varying severity that are swiftly sidestepped. The promise of leisure for future discussion offers hope that these things will be faced in an appropriate timescale, but it also heightens attention on unresolved things in the play. Shakespeare has shown a marvellous event, and has equipped the audience with the facts for a cynical response to the spectacle. The visual impact can hold sway if we want it to, but it is clearly in conflict with another way of reading the scene.

Shakespeare repeatedly features this conflict between a wonderful vision at the consummation of a romance, and the sense of intellectual anxiety caused by improbability and machination. It is worth wondering why Shakespeare might set up such an unresolved conclusion as that of *The Winter's Tale*. It does seem to be an interest at home in the late work of an author, since it enables reflection and meditation on the power in the dramatist's hands. There is also a generic factor, which is that romance supplies the perfect preconditions for such a meditation. And there is a profound thematic and emblematic connection between Truth and Time, where Truth is the daughter of Time, and proverbially 'time reveals all'. (It is worth remembering that the subtitle of *Pandosto* is *The Triumph of Time*; Shakespeare has made a great deal from this reference to the providential shape of the story.) An emblem in Geffrey Whitney's *A Choise of Emblems* (1586) shows Time bringing his daughter Truth into light. The emblem is suggestive in many ways for Shakespeare's late work—the unfolding of time, the relationship of father and daughter, and the emphasis on the visible appearance and recognition of truth. This is significant throughout the late plays, including *Henry VIII*, wherein daughters are seen again as the conduits for truth. This puts heightened emphasis on the nature of the truth of what is seen at the end of the play. That which is revealed may be in various senses false—Hermione is not a statue, the actress is not Hermione—but in the grander scheme of time something truer has been revealed. One kind of belief might outweigh the other. In representing stories that recall an emblematic connection, but do not just act it out, they may draw attention to the artificiality and contrivance required to present such a notion. The nexus of truth and time, of seeing and believing, shows Shakespeare advancing, and returning to, a powerful and substantial structuring certainty both in truth and in the idea that it can be seen and believed. Yet it also shows how Shakespeare engages the audience's capacity for thought and thus for doubt. In the end the vital thing is that the romances excite both wonder and reason, defying the possibility that they exclude one another.

Another factor is a developing mode of drama in Shakespeare's time, found not on the public stage but in the court theatre. In the court of James I an existing tradition—the presentation of mythical scenes in praise of the monarch, especially when provincial nobles and townspeople were striving to impress him or her—was enhanced and centralized. On festive occasions enormous resources were expended on courtly masques. These were written by leading writers (not Shakespeare, but his rival Ben Jonson was a leading exponent), employed professional actors but also courtiers in their casts, and usually told stories with a mythological and allegorical flavour that sought to flatter the monarch. The limited action and erudite messages were enhanced by music and visual spectacle. Designers such as Inigo Jones used ambitious technology and lavish budgets to present impressive scenes. This advance in the practical possibilities of the theatre connects with the themes of this chapter. As Anne Barton put it in an essay about the growing realism of the late plays, 'in a theatre with technical resources comparatively recently developed, the plot material to which Shakespeare now seems to have been drawn encouraged him to re-think the function of the eye in determining belief'.[4] Key scenes in the late romances, and indeed in *The Two*

Noble Kinsmen and *Henry VIII*, are closely related to court masques: they embrace the visual impressiveness but also the fakeness of such display.

These masque-like moments in Shakespeare's late work make issues of seeing and believing central. They represent a considerable critical challenge as it seems as if, on the one hand, these are scenes that might lack great significance or effectuality in the plays, and yet they are dramatically imposing. The energy expended on them is out of proportion and the audience or readers may feel this, but this does not mean that they fall flat. Rather they require attention to the things that they do not achieve, and to what elements of the play actually do achieve these things. One such is the arrival of Jupiter in *Cymbeline*. Up to a point this represents the restoration of Posthumus's fortunes, and with the god's blessing all will soon be well. Despite an impressive entrance, there is a feeling that this arrival serves a spectacular purpose first and foremost:

> *Jupiter descends in thunder and lightning, sitting*
> *upon an eagle. He throws a thunderbolt. The ghosts*
> *fall on their knees*

JUPITER

No more, you petty spirits of region low,
   Offend our hearing. Hush! How dare you ghosts
Accuse the thunderer, whose bolt, you know,
   Sky-planted, batters all rebelling coasts?
Poor shadows of Elysium, hence, and rest
   Upon your never-withering banks of flowers.
Be not with mortal accidents oppressed;
   No care of yours it is; you know 'tis ours.
Whom best I love, I cross, to make my gift,
   The more delayed, delighted. Be content.
Your low-laid son our godhead will uplift.
   His comforts thrive, his trials well are spent.
Our Jovial star reigned at his birth, and in
   Our temple was he married. Rise, and fade.

(5.5.187–200)

The image of Jupiter descending from above is aesthetically, thematically, and technologically akin to things happening in the court masque at this time. The closest surviving court analogy for the *Cymbeline* scene comes in the Inigo Jones designs for Aurelian Townshend's *Tempe Restored* (1632).[5] There is an even closer analogy in a play from the populist Red Bull theatre, Thomas Heywood's *The Golden Age* (1610/11), in the final scene of which Jupiter wins the throne of Olympus, is given his eagle, and ascends into Heaven.[6] Technology and thematic interests very likely did not only move from the court to the public stage; it is also interesting to consider whether the scene in *Cymbeline* led to that in *The Golden Age*, or even vice versa. Theatre historians tend to think that there was a complex conversation between the private and public theatres, as might be expected given the number of personnel involved in both.[7] An important extra element in the connection with masques is that (as Leah Marcus has explored) an iconographic connection between King James and Jupiter adds to the possible Jacobean interests of *Cymbeline*.[8] This gains a sharp edge if one feels that Jupiter makes a rather brash intrusion into the play, coming from nowhere and claiming a structuring authority in which it is somewhat hard to believe.

For in the *Cymbeline* scene there is a slight discrepancy between the grand and dismissive tone of his dealings with the 'petty spirits of region low', and the epigrammatic and even slightly glib 'Whom best I love, I cross, to make my gift, | The more delayed, delighted'. One way in which this is not epigrammatic is that it does not fill a couplet—as if the rather trite notion it offers cannot quite sustain the whole of two lines. His departure strikes a different odd note:

> JUPITER   Mount, eagle, to my palace crystalline.
> > *He ascends into the heavens*
> SICILIUS   He came in thunder. His celestial breath
> Was sulphurous to smell. The holy eagle
> Stooped, as to foot us. His ascension is
> More sweet than our blest fields. His royal bird
> Preens the immortal wing, and claws his beak
> As when his god is pleased.
> ALL   Thanks, Jupiter.
> SICILIUS   The marble pavement closes, he is entered
> His radiant roof. Away, and, to be blest,
> Let us with care perform his great behest.

> (5.5.207–16)

Every detail in Shakespeare's description runs the risk of evoking a strange rather than impressive image. The eagle's actions seem oddly matched with its role as carriage. The sulphurous breath may have been accompanied by an audience laugh at the result of some stage pyrotechnics—an acrid cloud. Even without this it lingers on a physical detail that only with considerable effort really seems majestic. So the appearance of Jupiter is oddly pitched. But this is in proportion with what he actually leaves behind, namely a prophecy which is interpreted by a Soothsayer some time later:

> 'Whenas a lion's whelp shall, to himself unknown, without seeking find, and be embraced by a piece of tender air; and when from a stately cedar shall be lopped branches which, being dead many years, shall after revive, be jointed to the old stock, and freshly grow: then shall Posthumus end his miseries, Britain be fortunate and flourish in peace and plenty.'

(5.5.232–8)

> Thou, Leonatus, art the lion's whelp.
> The fit and apt construction of thy name,
> Being *leo-natus*, doth import so much.
> (*To Cymbeline*) The piece of tender air thy virtuous daughter,
> Which we call '*mollis aer*'; and '*mollis aer*'
> We term it '*mulier*', (*to Posthumus*) which '*mulier*' I divine
> Is this most constant wife, who even now,
> Answering the letter of the oracle,
> Unknown to you, unsought, were clipped about
> With this most tender air.

(5.6.436–53)

Again it is difficult to know how to read this: to some extent this is the culmination of the providential plot of the play, and yet when Jupiter's gift is finally interpreted it merely retells things that have already been established. The identification of Leonatus with the 'lion's whelp' is very obvious. The pedantic etymology of *mulier* (woman/wife) is forced and even comical. Since the play hints only vaguely at classical gods providing a providential underpinning to the action, it does seem as if one might read Jupiter to be overplaying his significance in things.

This also seems to be the case in other masque-like scenes where gods appear, or are mentioned, in Shakespearian romance. The exception might be *The Two Noble Kinsmen*, where both heroes pray (to Mars and Venus respectively) and have their prayers rewarded. Nevertheless, the barefaced nature of the conclusion, where the one who prayed to Mars wins the battle, but the one who prayed to Venus wins love, puts more attention on the boldness of the storytelling than on the power of the gods. This, indeed, may be a common theme: while Shakespeare does appropriate the energy and spectacle of masque scenes, and introduces a numinous and weighty note to the plays, the figures wheeled on (or flown in) never really command the providential order of the plays. Hence the energy and spectacle, the numinous and weighty notes, gather around the power of the play and the creator behind it—or possibly, as the next chapter explores, behind a generalized Christian spirituality. In *Pericles* the order of things means that the divine revelation that Thaisa is in Diana's temple, and the reunion of husband and wife, make a fitting conclusion to the play, but are dwarfed by proximity to the un-divine recognition of father and daughter in 5.1. In *The Winter's Tale* the most masque-like scene is 5.3, the statue scene, but there the presiding presences are all human; and Leontes ignores Apollo's oracle, though ultimately it proves true as a description of the play.

The final example is different because it is not simply a staging of a divine appearance. Instead, in *The Tempest* there is a staging of a staging of a divine appearance. Prospero arranges for his spirits to entertain Miranda and Ferdinand with a masque of three goddesses, and later some naiads and some reapers. The purpose of this is made explicit:

> CERES Hail, many-coloured messenger, that ne'er
>   Dost disobey the wife of Jupiter;
>   Who with thy saffron wings upon my flowers
>   Diffusest honey-drops, refreshing showers,
>   And with each end of thy blue bow dost crown
>   My bosky acres and my unshrubbed down,
>   Rich scarf to my proud earth. Why hath thy queen
>   Summoned me hither to this short-grassed green?
> IRIS A contract of true love to celebrate,
>   And some donation freely to estate
>   On the blest lovers.

(4.1.76–86)

The goddesses raise the linguistic temperature—'saffron wings', 'bosky acres'—but their business is a little opaque. While they may be there to celebrate the union of Ferdinand and Miranda up to a point, they are also there to emphasize and re-emphasize the fact that the lovers must remain chaste. To that end their function is partly to divert and detain the lovers in case of temptation. So the goddesses in *The Tempest* are, extraordinarily, there to fill up time—taking the sense of slight extraneousness found around classical gods in the other romances a stage further. Nevertheless Prospero wants attentive viewers:

> FERDINAND   Let me live here ever!
>   So rare a wondered father and a wise
>   Makes this place paradise.
>   *Juno and Ceres whisper, and send Iris on*
>   *employment*
> PROSPERO   Sweet now, silence.
>   Juno and Ceres whisper seriously.
>   There's something else to do. Hush, and be mute,
>   Or else our spell is marred.
> IRIS   You nymphs called naiads of the wind'ring brooks,
>   With your sedged crowns and ever-harmless looks,
>   Leave your crisp channels, and on this green land
>   Answer your summons; Juno does command.
>   Come, temperate nymphs, and help to celebrate
>   A contract of true love. Be not too late.
>
>   (4.1.122–33)

The spirits stick to an appropriate message under the careful eye of their master, and he hams up the tension resulting from Ferdinand's bland interruption. Soon afterwards the masque ends and Prospero becomes very troubled, and not only by the confederacy of Caliban that he suddenly remembers. The real action of the play is rather different from the decorous goddesses' pronouncements, and they look more and more like a backwater. Indeed, the masque ends in a romping dance of reapers which suggests sexuality and licence rather than chastity. The reapers also evoke death, a strange presence on such an occasion. So Prospero's show gets a little out of control, hinting at tensions and anxieties that run entirely against its ostensible purpose. Actually, this is a viable reading of numerous court masques, though they have their antimasques, the playful and irreverent bits, before the main action; this structure brings the antimasquers under control. The appearances of classical deities are never exactly doubted by the audience: they do not seem out of place within the world of Shakespearian romance, but they do not have much to contribute to the plots and characters. The world that can sustain them and the plots that enable their entry do not actually need them. Attention is shifted towards the true controlling powers of the play. However, Prospero's masque shows the limits of control: he sets his play in motion and it rebounds on him. This is a reflection on his project as a whole: he can raise a daughter, he can reconfigure the power dynamics of the Mediterranean, but he cannot control them wholly or forever. It also suggests a reflection on the nature of drama: it too has a life of its own and its initial creator must relinquish his possession once it takes bodily form. These things are vital and energetic, yet they are also accepted with a hint of sadness, when the dream of perfection is lost.

The Tempest is Shakespeare's most masque-like play and it is also the play where questions of seeing and believing get sharpest. It includes among its characters both the contriver of the marvellous visions, and very different audiences to witness them. It starts with a storm that must have been a *tour de force* of public stage technology, with special effects and frantic action. In the theatre this works best, I suggest, when it is done without explicit irony—without, for example, Prospero visibly orchestrating the storm. The arch example of this tendency is Peter Greenaway's film *Prospero's Books* (1991) wherein almost every line of the play is spoken by John Gielgud playing Prospero, and the storm is his illusory creation. In many ways this is a fine film, but it loses the important opportunity to juxtapose the candid intensity of that first scene with the second, where we find that others have been watching the sailors suffer:

> MIRANDA   If by your art, my dearest father, you have
> Put the wild waters in this roar, allay them.
> The sky, it seems, would pour down stinking pitch,
> But that the sea, mounting to th' welkin's cheek,
> Dashes the fire out. O, I have sufferèd
> With those that I saw suffer! A brave vessel,
> Who had, no doubt, some noble creature in her,
> Dashed all to pieces! O, the cry did knock

Against my very heart! Poor souls, they perished.
Had I been any god of power, I would
Have sunk the sea within the earth, or ere
It should the good ship so have swallowed and
The fraughting souls within her.
PROSPERO   Be collected.
No more amazement. Tell your piteous heart
There's no harm done.

(1.2.1–15)

Miranda's response has two contradictory components. On the one
hand, she knows that such things have been arranged by her father
before, so there is hope. On the other, she is moved and shocked
by what she has seen. This contradiction is at the heart of viewing
a play: an awareness of artifice and an emotional engagement work
together. However, in *The Tempest* her reaction, and her father's
reassurance, have other ramifications. When she compares herself to
a 'god of power' able to undo what has occurred, she strikes up an
uncomfortable comparison for her father, who is able to do and undo
such things—Prospero's power could be associated with good or bad
magic, with benign or dangerous influences, and it could be too great.
Most of all, it is interesting to consider whether the ability to be
both ironically aware and emotionally affected is actually admirable in
an onstage character. In an audience, it is a necessary and generous
paradox; in the daughter of a magician, it looks like self-indulgence.
This is additionally the case because this second scene so radically
overturns the dynamics of the first: where we heard desperate offstage
cries and even saw 'Mariners, wet', now we are comfortably on the
shore, spectators to an illusion within an illusion.

Throughout *The Tempest* the audience sees characters frightened,
deluded, or entertained by noises and spirits, banquets and masques.
We see how they watch, with varying degrees of awareness, a series
of partial analogies for the play we ourselves are witnessing. There is
also the figure of the magician, who arranges them. It is possible to
overstretch the identification of Prospero with a dramatist, or with
Shakespeare himself, but this facet of the character is significant, in
that (as with Miranda as a figure of the audience above) key issues
in the nature of drama appear rather different when played out on
the stage. The modern tendency to see Prospero as a tyrannical

ruler, at least as much as an ideal one, sharpens the metatheatrical element. It also helps explain the difference in *The Tempest*'s version of the dynamics of seeing and believing, of participating in wonder and undermining it with reason. For in this play Prospero's view dominates, and his interpretation of events stifles resistance to it. In the end even Caliban recognizes the folly of opposition.

However, any magician should accept that part of the attraction of his show is the thought that it can be discredited. There is no obvious vent for that activity in the play, so the possibilities of resistant interpretation are pursued elsewhere. And *The Tempest* does contain a number of viewpoints which resist the exiled Duke, and which do so in relation to seeing and believing. The debate in 2.1 between Gonzalo's idealistic optimism and the crabbed cynicism of Antonio and Sebastian is not simply a tired exploration of the difference between hope and hate, between morally discernible world-pictures. When they snipe about whether the ground is 'green' or 'tawny' neither side's view can be verified with reference to facts. While Gonzalo offers a surer course through the play, at times it might seem like a less attractive one than that offered by the malignant courtiers, because at least theirs incorporates some freedom to judge outside Prospero's power.

The most important voice of resistance is Caliban. This is most obviously true when the play's colonial dynamics are taken into account. He is not only a recalcitrant primitive abused (or not) by a tyrant. He also displays a kind of poetry that is very much his own, though it appears only fleetingly.[9] The play does not give much access to his higher thoughts, because Prospero does not concede that he has any. Nevertheless these are not the words of a 'thing of darkness' in the derogatory sense used by the Duke:

CALIBAN   Art thou afeard?
STEFANO   No, monster, not I.
CALIBAN   Be not afeard. The isle is full of noises,
   Sounds, and sweet airs, that give delight and hurt not.
   Sometimes a thousand twangling instruments
   Will hum about mine ears, and sometime voices
   That if I then had waked after long sleep
   Will make me sleep again; and then in dreaming
   The clouds methought would open and show riches

> Ready to drop upon me, that when I waked
> I cried to dream again.
> STEFANO   This will prove a brave kingdom to me, where I shall have
> my music for nothing.
> CALIBAN   When Prospero is destroyed.
>
> (3.2.136–49)

Stefano the drunken sailor provides his own interpretation of that late Shakespearian keyword 'brave', describing a world where his creature comforts will be free. Caliban exists at a different level, moved by beauty and the loss of beauty, and moving us with the image of waking in tears. The word 'twangling' is intriguing: it tends to be used negatively, for an unpleasant note. This is not how Caliban uses it—and a similar point could be made about 'hum'. These words are his special music, and they suggest an aesthetic sensibility that lies outside Prospero's control. Hence it may operate as a saving grace in the play—an antidote to the dominance of the world-view of Prospero. It is worth saying here that to expose and endorse hints of resistance to Prospero in the play does not necessarily require disapproval of everything or even anything he does; this is a play about the problematic action of power in the real world, and the illusory world of the island turns out to be an ideal place to encounter the fact that power must inevitably face compromises with reality. Being realistic about the difficulty of government might actually make one sympathetic to governors (but it might not), even as one recognizes their abuses and deceits.

The individual nature of Caliban's language is evident earlier in the play, where he uses a word—'seamews' in the Oxford edition, 'scamels' in the Folio—that has perplexed editors. There is much merit in the suggestion that 'scamel' is a misreading of the manuscript which had 'seamel', a variant spelling of 'seamew', which is an old name for a seagull.[10] However, the (understandable) premiss behind that emendation is that each character's speech should be as lucid as possible. It could also be argued that Caliban displays reserves of strange imagination and intellectual independence that might suit some opaque vocabulary. A 'scamel' on its own is a problem, but in context it becomes part of the native food of the island and its meaning is less of an issue. It contributes thereby to the development of Caliban's unusual voice, and to the questions of seeing and believing in the island. Now it is part of only one dweller's special vision:

> I prithee, let me bring thee where crabs grow,
> And I with my long nails will dig thee pig-nuts,
> Show thee a jay's nest, and instruct thee how
> To snare the nimble marmoset. I'll bring thee
> To clust'ring filberts, and sometimes I'll get thee
> Young scamels [seamews] from the rock. Wilt thou go with me?
>
> (2.2.166–71)

Even with the 'seamews' this shows Caliban's island rather than anyone else's. In the Folio this speech is actually set out as prose. It was Pope's edition in the early eighteenth century that recovered, or discovered, or indeed invented, the poetry of these lines. They do not scan perfectly by any means, and this is not one of the many clear cases in the Folio of mislineation. Nevertheless the versification of these lines becomes part of a redefinition of the character and his language. The final phrase, 'wilt thou go with me?', compounds the lyrical quality: it sounds almost like a love-poem, which further measures the gap in sensibility between Caliban and his listeners, Stefano and Trinculo. His vocabulary, like 'twangling' above, suggests an alternative way of looking at the world. His vision of 'crabs', 'pig-nuts', 'marmosets', and most of all 'scamels', is not the same island as Prospero's.

The Tempest represents a change in the relationship of seeing and believing. In *Antony and Cleopatra* and *The Winter's Tale* the power of the poetry, the visual spectacle, and the emotional drive of the play seem to dare the reader or viewer to reject the objections of cynicism and rationalism. In *The Tempest* we see the action controlled before our eyes, and while the essentially pleasurable outcome still has power, Prospero's methods of control do not breed trust. Notes of resistance in the play, which defy the authority of the artist, assume greater importance not because they undermine the future happiness of Miranda and Ferdinand, but because they demonstrate our chances to read and see what Prospero does not want us to. Throughout Shakespeare's late work there is a constant interest in how audiences watch the action. To some extent we are tempted towards the certainties offered by wonder; if we believe what we see then we are admitted to the aesthetic and moral values of romance. However, we are always equipped with the facts and theories to undermine the wondrous visions—any decision to participate is conscious and aware, and the active pleasure of suspending disbelief is never taken out of our hands.

Faith and Revelation

In Shakespeare's late work characters find things that are terribly important to them; in this chapter broader ramifications of the theme of finding and discovery will be examined. In these works it often seems as if grand, powerful ideas are being put forward, ideas that promise rejuvenation and new security. However, these new directions are not proposed without being questioned, and a rich ironic texture results. One of these sets of ideas is a religious and spiritual one, and this version of discovery has a particular intensity in *Pericles*, not least because the play itself also seems to enact and indeed to be a kind of discovery. It is usually seen as the earliest of the romances, and has a position therefore at a kind of dividing line in Shakespeare's career. For it to be seen as a genuine starting-point in a larger sense, a first step (or a forerunner) of a new direction, it needs to have some other features that communicate its difference and its novelty. Things are made more complicated by the fact that *Pericles* is partly by George Wilkins, which hampers any argument about Shakespearian innovation, and which causes more simple problems to the reader trying to unscramble the text of a patchy Quarto printed in 1609.[1] In addition, *Pericles* is not included in the 1623 First Folio edition, which casts circumstantial doubt on its centrality in any account of Shakespeare's work.

However, the problems of the text and authorship of *Pericles* form part of the experience of reading the play, and they contribute to the feeling that it does indeed represent a new departure. It is hard to read without focusing on certain moments of trauma and discovery, moments that seem to have greater intensity than is required by the plot, an impression that is actually helped by the uncertainties that haunt the play. Such peaks of disproportionate intensity may lead the reader to feel that other things are being lost and found in this text. Accordingly it is possible to present *Pericles* as the first last play, a play founded on its own struggle to become itself, and to achieve its own conclusion. If some of this is derived from hindsight and knowledge of Shakespearian chronology and the text's doubtful authorship, this is not an insoluble difficulty. One cannot un-know such things, and it might be a risky critical practice to do so. This does not mean that one cannot question the authorship problem, but it does mean that the problems of *Pericles* are as fundamental to many modern readings of this play as the problems of Pericles.

The usual dividing point between non-Shakespearian and Shakespearian material is the beginning of Scene 11. After ten scenes of another writer's work, Shakespeare takes over. It is fitting, then, that Act 3 starts with a moment of crisis as Pericles faces a storm that seems to herald more than a change of location:

> The god of this great vast rebuke these surges
> Which wash both heav'n and hell; and thou that hast
> Upon the winds command, bind them in brass,
> Having called them from the deep. O still
> Thy deaf'ning dreadful thunders, gently quench
> Thy nimble sulph'rous flashes—O, ho, Lychorida!
> How does my queen?—Thou stormest venomously.
> Wilt thou spit all thyself? The seaman's whistle
> Is as a whisper in the ears of death,
> Unheard.—Lychorida!—Lucina, O!
> Divinest patroness, and midwife gentle
> To those that cry by night, convey thy deity
> Aboard our dancing boat, make swift the pangs
> Of my queen's travails!—Now, Lychorida.
>
> (Scene 11, 1–14)

There are problems with the text of the Quarto that later editors have ironed out. In the case of *Pericles* it is useful to keep track of difficulties with the original text, as they are part of the full complexity of the play. The Quarto has the meaningless 'my wife' in line 11, emended by the perceptive eighteenth-century editor George Steevens to 'midwife'. The emendment is appropriate because the Roman moon goddess Lucina was worshipped for her role in offering comfort to women in labour. The image of the surging waves which 'wash both heav'n and hell', that word 'wash' both disarmingly gentle and powerfully purifying, is arresting. It suggests that this storm is no mere punctuation mark in an episodic play; the hero is undergoing part of a process of spiritual renewal. The fearsome god is asked to quench his lightning 'gently', a far from obvious word which reflects the way that this speech seems to want to calm the storm to gentleness through its own words. Thus the boat is 'dancing'. 'Gentle' occurs again in the invocation of Lucina, but it is the phrase 'that cry by night' which is most noteworthy. It evokes the pains of childbirth, but other kinds of solitary pain happening under the moon are evoked, and this from a character who is involved throughout the play in a spiritual night and a sad dream. The violent image of the storm spitting its whole self is a mind-twisting picture of natural violence. The last image to mention is that of 'the seaman's whistle' which 'is as a whisper in the ears of death, unheard'. The combination of the frantic noise of the storm, which drowns out the piercing whistle, with the unhearing and also silent image of death, provides a remarkable shift of focus. So the language of this speech embodies the scene it is describing, and of course it is creating the scene at the same time.

The storm at sea is also a storm of language, conveyed not (as in *The Tempest*) by the hubbub of activity and frantic commands, but by a set-piece speech. For a modern reader it could be seen to mark a crisis point not only in the hero's journey, but also in the play's progress, and indeed in its composition: this, after all, is probably Shakespeare's arrival in the text, so it may also be an announcement of his presence. (Clearly it is unwise to assume that speeches are written in their scene order, but the point is more about how the writing seems than how it might actually have happened.) The point acquires greater focus when the Scene II storm speech is compared with another similar moment six scenes earlier:

> Yet cease your ire, you angry stars of heaven!
> Wind, rain, and thunder, remember earthly man
> Is but a substance that must yield to you,
> And I, as fits my nature, do obey you.
> Alas, the seas hath cast me on the rocks,
> Washed me from shore to shore, and left my breath
> Nothing to think on but ensuing death.

> Let it suffice the greatness of your powers
> To have bereft a prince of all his fortunes,
> And, having thrown him from your wat'ry grave,
> Here to have death in peace is all he'll crave.

> (Scene 5, 41–51)

This too is a pivotal moment in the plot, as the fortunes of Pericles take another turn. The Scene 11 storm featured a crucial birth and a crucial death—the prince's wife Thaisa apparently dies in childbirth—but the contrast between the two storm speeches is not solely explicable in plot terms. Here the syntax and structure are nothing like as storm-tossed. The language is sterile in comparison with the relentless fertility of the other. The address to the storm works through a conventional gesture of deference to nature without really giving it any special energy. The contrast with the other storm speech suggests that the Scene 11 example does indeed represent a greater rift in the play than is determined by the plot. So there may be a special moment of traumatic arrival in *Pericles* as Shakespeare takes over the play, using an excessively pivotal speech as a coded way of announcing his presence; so at least it may seem to readers and audiences of romances who know that storms come at critical junctures, as in *The Tempest* and *The Winter's Tale*.

The Scene 11 storm is not the only scene in *Pericles* that offers intensity beyond the range of the rest of the play. The long recognition scene (Scene 21) is in some ways conventional—recognition scenes are found in a remarkable range of dramatic forms, and are very much at home in romance, which lends itself to powerful moments where mysteries are solved. In the late plays the recognition scene undergoes various mutations, with *The Winter's Tale* in particular offering two vastly different treatments. In one case, the reunion of father and daughter happens offstage and is narrated by three gentlemen whose witty and detached perspective provides us with an unusual viewpoint. The second, when King Leontes 'recognizes' that the statue before him has become his wife, is very different, with the audience given no barrier between it and the amazed joy of the central character. But the scene in *Pericles* is an endurance test: the abject King moves painstakingly through the process of working out that the girl in front of him is the daughter he thought had died. The lingering detail of the revelation is protracted to an extent not equalled anywhere else in

Shakespeare. There is something of the gradualness of the resolution
of loss in *Twelfth Night*, but without the absoluteness of the hero's
erstwhile despair.[2] Pericles' thirst for information contrasts poignantly
with his reluctance to accept the truth:

PERICLES   Tell thy story.
   If thine considered prove the thousandth part
   Of my endurance, thou art a man, and I
   Have suffered like a girl. Yet thou dost look
   Like patience gazing on kings' graves, and smiling
   Extremity out of act. What were thy friends?
   How lost thou them? Thy name, my most kind virgin?
   Recount, I do beseech thee. Come, sit by me.
      She sits
MARINA   My name, sir, is Marina.
PERICLES   O, I am mocked,
   And thou by some incensèd god sent hither
   To make the world to laugh at me.

              (Scene 21, 123–33)

In the moments leading up to this, Pericles has been at first immovable,
and then, when Marina's remarkable resemblance to his lost wife
becomes clear, inquisitive. The process by which the details emerge
is a tortured one, with the King's keen sense of persecution haunting
him, making him fear even the best news. In fearing that he is being
mocked by a cruel god Pericles resembles Lear—a connection explored
in the first chapter of this book. As the truth comes out, it does so in
fits and starts, outmanoeuvring the questions. Pericles is portrayed as
not ready for the good news, lost in his own suffering. His image of
patience smiling on kings' graves absorbs our attention too. The grand
perspective it offers—personified patience recognizes the smallness of
the death of kings and worldly affairs, and smiles—is arresting, and
gives an insight into how Pericles' philosophical response to suffering
has actually hardened him to good news as well as bad. The crucial
question, which in some ways should reveal all, is an afterthought,
and its answer interpreted within the dark world of Pericles' troubles.

   The discovery is protracted partly because the hero is incapable
of processing the information. Terence Cave, in his brilliant study
of recognition scenes, explores a psychological and psychoanalyti-
cal approach when discussing *Pericles*.[3] This character's trials and

tribulations do indeed have this quality: his ability to deal with the world has been compromised by trauma. It fits with this approach that Pericles tries to put the amazing events in a comprehensible context by imagining his life as a dream:

> O, stop there a little! [*Aside*] This is the rarest dream
> That e'er dulled sleep did mock sad fools withal.
> This cannot be my daughter, buried. Well.
> (*To Marina*) Where were you bred? I'll hear you more to th' bottom
> Of your story, and never interrupt you.

> (Scene 21, 149–53)

Later editors have often added the direction that this should be spoken 'aside' (a modification to the Quarto originally made by Edmond Malone),[4] which is really an unnecessary change, perhaps reflecting the awkwardness of watching this scene. A tortured private pain is being expiated in public; watching it happen is voyeuristic not least because we know that we expect everything to turn out well. Having Pericles voice these awkward sentiments aside gets over the problem that in suggesting that he might be Marina's father he is jumping the gun, as far as she is concerned. She knows nothing of what will transpire. But that awkwardness could be appropriate, as this dishevelled man, mumbling rubbish, actually holds the truth. As Marina unfolds her story the wonderful news begins to emerge, until the ritual of identification reaches its climax. Marina finally asks Pericles for his name:

> PERICLES   I am Pericles
> Of Tyre. But tell me now my drowned queen's name.
> As in the rest thou hast been godlike perfect,
> So prove but true in that, thou art my daughter,
> The heir of kingdoms, and another life
> To Pericles thy father.
> MARINA[*kneeling*]   Is it no more
> To be your daughter than to say my mother's name?
> Thaisa was my mother, who did end
> The minute I began.
> PERICLES   Now blessing upon thee. Rise. Thou art my child.
>   [*Marina stands. He kisses her*]
>   [*To attendants*] Give me fresh garments.

> (Scene 21, 191–201)

In line 195 the Quarto has 'an other like'; 'another life' is Steevens's choice, while Malone preferred 'a mother like'. Either of these emendations makes Marina into a regenerative force in her father's life, paradoxically giving him life. The Oxford edition makes some significant changes in this exchange. Line 194 is a new line, added to fill a gap in sense. The Quarto also has Marina say her mother's name twice: 'Is it no more to be your daughter than | To say my mother's name was Thaisa? | Thaisa was my mother'. It is sound enough to argue that this is typical of 'memorial expansion and duplication', to which this text is prone elsewhere. However, this change is both less necessary than the addition of line 194, and loses something.[5] The talismanic repetition of the name of the mother—although fathers and daughters may dominate the plots of the late plays, mothers are powerful forces whether present or absent—makes even more of the final piece in the jigsaw. With fresh garments, Pericles will begin 'another life'.

Shakespeare gives a powerful picture of how a fragmented self becomes reintegrated as the parts of his life, scattered over the Mediterranean, are rejoined. It might be possible to detect a naive but telling incredulity at the rigours of recognition in Marina's wondering 'Is it no more | To be your daughter than to say my mother's name?' Since others onstage do not share the intensity of recognition felt by Pericles, there is further reason to explore whether the audience may be aware of its own distance from this intensity as it works within the scene. On the one hand, this is an extremely moving moment in the theatre and on the page; no point about the audience's perspective will question its essential effectiveness. On the other, there is an introverted quality to the hero's emotion: we watch with Marina as he is swallowed up in joy and relief. Thus here, as elsewhere in the play, there may be a reason for inferring an internal agenda. There may be another story being told or experienced alongside *Pericles*. It is probably wise here, as with *The Tempest*, to retain a sceptical position as regards the self-referential quality of the play. What I am trying to outline is a drift in interpretation that the play makes possible, rather than its meaning. Paradoxically, the recognition scene is so inwardly intense that it might appear to be recognizing things outside the play. Pericles is transported even further by the final revelation of the scene:

PERICLES   Give me my robes.
          [*He is attired in fresh robes*]
                                        I am wild in my beholding.
      O heavens, bless my girl!
          [*Celestial music*]
                                        But hark, what music?
      Tell Helicanus, my Marina, tell him
      O'er point by point, for yet he seems to doubt,
      How sure you are my daughter. But what music?
HELICANUS   My lord, I hear none.
PERICLES   None? The music of the spheres! List, my Marina.

                                        (Scene 21, 209–15)

Diana then appears and tells him that Thaisa is at her temple in
Ephesus. At this stage, however, Pericles is briefly incoherent, and
could be heading for a revelation as fragile as Lear's momentary vision
of Cordelia's revival in the Folio version of *King Lear* (5.3.286–7). Here
it seems possible to say that the great recognition scene proves too
much for its human hero in a number of senses: too much because he
swoons and, apparently unhinged, hears music, and too much because
even after all this there is still more to come. (The stage direction
'*Celestial music*' is not there in the Quarto, so it is possible to play this
scene without it, and in that case Pericles would seem all the more
transported. He is not deluded, since the vision is true. The question
is how much we are admitted within his reverie.) As in *The Winter's
Tale*, the recovery of one lost thing leads to the recovery of others.
Scene 21 (in the Oxford edition; the significantly placed Act 5 Scene
1 in others) focuses so much energy on the difficulty of its discovery
that it exceeds the plot. The rest of the play hardly seems to support
the painstaking, and pains-causing, protraction of this scene. It acts
on the spectator like an invitation to imagine what might be going on
in this play, outside the action.

   Some speculative kinds of external story can result from the identification of this kind of excessive intensity. It should be acknowledged,
though, that it is a common and natural habit of reading to think about
texts in relation to their authors' lives. *Pericles* plays a fulcrum role in
a boldly inclusive sketch of Shakespeare's career by E. K. Chambers.
Written in 1930, its technique is not what would be categorized today
as sound scholarship, but it is definitely a good story:

The temper of *Hamlet* and *Troilus and Cressida* leads up, naturally enough, to the long unfolding of the Jacobean tragedies. These are not without evidence of mental strain and sometimes exhaustion. Shakespeare's spirit must have been nearly submerged in *Lear*, and although the wave passed, and he rose to his height of poetic expression in *Antony and Cleopatra*, I think that he went under in the unfinished *Timon of Athens*. The chronology of the plays becomes difficult at this point, and it is therefore frankly a conjecture that an attempt at *Timon of Athens* early in 1608 was followed by a serious illness, which may have been a nervous breakdown, and on the other hand may have been merely the plague. Later in the same year Shakespeare came to his part of *Pericles* with a new outlook. In any case the transition from the tragedies to the romances is not an evolution but a revolution. There has been some mental process such as the psychology of religion would call a conversion. Obviously the philosophy of the tragedies is not a Christian philosophy, and in a sense that of the romances is.[6]

Chambers says it may have been a nervous breakdown, or, 'merely the plague'. Now 'merely' does not seem the obvious word to use around this disease. This reminds us of two things: one, that the idea of Shakespeare had been refined so far by this point that any infringement of his mental capacity vastly outweighs a terrifying physical ailment. The other thing it reminds us is that 1607 and 1608 were plague years, and the theatres in London spent much time closed. This may have given Shakespeare the time to think again about his Sonnets, which came out in 1609, as he had turned to poetry (*Venus and Adonis* and *Lucrece*) during other plague closures in the 1590s. It also may represent a physical and material reason why the predominant style of his plays changed: for the reopening Shakespeare was perhaps refreshed, or faced an audience with different interests and demands. But this is biographical speculation, making tenuous connections between a poorly documented life and an enigmatic text—which is what Chambers is doing as well.

Whichever theory of authorship is believed, there is a strong tendency to see *Pericles* as an uneven work. Other critics have tried to give the play a more artistic coherence. One clearly important way of doing so is to emphasize its emblematic structure. Claire Preston sees the scenes as part of a deeply symbolic, episodic narrative; the unusual structure of *Pericles* reflects a different kind of storytelling from Shakespeare's usual narrative-based mode.[7] It could be seen as a medieval-style, ritualistic progress, where the dramaturgy changes to fit new settings and action. F. D. Hoeniger has developed a similar point in relation to the role of Gower in the play.[8] He sees the changes in tone as part of an attempt to recover an old style of storytelling to suit new circumstances. Elsewhere, he has explored the connection between *Pericles* and medieval miracle plays, explaining thereby the diverse spiritual moods and the episodic structure—miracle plays told the stories of the saints in a series of segments, often with very different genres.[9] Hoeniger's argument starts with the idea that it is possible for us to overrate differences in style because in the pace of performance these would be glossed over. This is important in the history of the play, because its notable popularity in the seventeenth century will hardly have been because of its intriguing unevenness. However, for a critic it is perhaps an abdication of responsibility to explain the play in terms of such a limited perspective. It is first and foremost a dramatic entity, but one can still assume an audience adept enough to follow the poetry, as opposed to one that cannot.

The peaks and troughs of the play do not necessarily mean that it is the congruence of two separate designs. It is instructive to think about how things are sometimes shared between the two halves of the play, partly belying the idea of separateness. There are numerous scenes throughout *Pericles* that evoke other late plays. A good example of the 'lateness' of *Pericles* is the scene in which Cerimon, the physician on the shore at Ephesus, revives Thaisa. It features magic, a transition from death to life that is not quite what it seems, and music. It has a lot in common with the revival of Hermione at the end of *The Winter's Tale*:

> CERIMON Well said, well said, the fire and cloths.
>   The still and woeful music that we have,
>   Cause it to sound, beseech you.
>   *Music*
>   The vial once more.
>   How thou stirr'st, thou block! The music there!
>   I pray you give her air. Gentlemen,
>   This queen will live. Nature awakes, a warmth
>   Breathes out of her. She hath not been entranced
>   Above five hours. See how she 'gins to blow
>   Into life's flow'r again!

FIRST GENTLEMAN   The heavens
   Through you increase our wonder, and set up
   Your fame for ever.
CERIMON   She is alive. Behold,
   Her eyelids, cases to those heav'nly jewels
   Which Pericles hath lost,
   Begin to part their fringes of bright gold.
   The diamonds of a most praisèd water
   Doth appear to make the world twice rich.—Live,
   And make us weep to hear your fate, fair creature,
   Rare as you seem to be.
     She moves.
THAISA   O dear Diana,
   Where am I? Where's my lord? What world is this?
SECOND GENTLEMAN   Is not this strange?
FIRST GENTLEMAN   Most rare.

(Scene 12, 85–104)

The Quarto has 'Violl' in line 92, but the emendation to 'vial' surely makes sense; it is interesting, though, how the simultaneous music and medicine match a slippage of language.[10] The second gentleman is right that this scene is 'strange', although this word (like his colleague's 'rare') is used with its special late Shakespearian intonation, where the strange is also the marvellous. When Thaisa wakes and asks 'what world is this?' the question is a good one; Cerimon has brought her back to life through medicine, but Shakespeare is careful to point out that she 'hath not been entranced above five hours'—it is not actually a resurrection. But of course it is, from Pericles' point of view, and also to a considerable extent from ours. As with the amazing coming-to-life of Hermione's statue, we can make use of a simple and prosaic explanation if that is what we really want, but the tempting possibilities of wonderful events are tellingly attractive.

Music plays as Cerimon works. Even his name hints at a new sort of 'ceremonial' scene, in which narrative time (like Thaisa's life) is temporarily suspended. This alteration in the fabric of onstage reality is characteristic of Shakespearian romance. The presence of music in an early scene in the play, before the watershed of Scene 12, should alert us to the fact that scenes reminiscent of late Shakespeare appear throughout the text we have:

ANTIOCHUS   Music!
> *Music sounds*
Bring in our daughter, clothèd like a bride
Fit for th'embracements ev'n of Jove himself,
At whose conception, till Lucina reigned,
Nature this dowry gave to glad her presence:
The senate-house of planets all did sit,
In her their best perfections to knit.
> *Enter Antiochus' Daughter*
PERICLES   See where she comes, apparelled like the spring,
Graces her subjects, and her thoughts the king
Of ev'ry virtue gives renown to men;
Her face the book of praises, where is read
Nothing but curious pleasures, as from thence
Sorrow were ever razed and testy wrath
Could never be her mild companion.

(Scene 1, 48–61)

The Quarto of 1609 begins Antiochus' first line with 'Musicke bring in our daughter', which breaks the scansion and is rather opaque.[11] In the late eighteenth century Malone came up with an obvious but nevertheless clever solution that the word 'music' must have been a stage direction, perhaps added late to a manuscript and easily confused with the dialogue when the printer came to set the page. In the Oxford edition the word is retained as part of the dialogue, but is accompanied by a necessary stage direction. The version above helps seal the connection between this scene and other late plays, recalling Paulina's line 'Music; awake her; strike!' that heralds the transformation of Hermione (*The Winter's Tale* 5.3.94).

Pericles' rapt attention when seeing Antiochus' daughter is distinctively 'late' in character. The phrase 'apparelled like the spring', the reference to her 'graces', and indeed the way that she accumulates 'subjects', all recall descriptions of heroines in the late plays, but particularly Perdita in *The Winter's Tale*, as she queens it in the pastoral feast of Act 4 Scene 4. As was mentioned in the first chapter, this is one of those features of Shakespearian romance that John Jones believes were removed from the Folio *Lear*. Such connections are all the stronger in the case of Marina, who comes in the 'Shakespearian' second part of the play. She is depicted bringing flowers to her nurse's grave:

MARINA   No, I will rob Tellus of her weed
    To strew thy grave with flow'rs. The yellows, blues,
    The purple violets and marigolds
    Shall as a carpet hang upon thy tomb
    While summer days doth last. Ay me, poor maid,
    Born in a tempest when my mother died,
    This world to me is but a ceaseless storm
    Whirring me from my friends.

(Scene 15, 65–72)[12]

The final two lines combine the grand importance of Marina's fate (the world imagined as a 'ceaseless storm'), the chaos of environment and of language ('whirring'), and her own humble perspective (the loss of her 'friends'). Perdita in *The Winter's Tale* and Innogen in *Cymbeline* are natural comparisons for Marina here as they too link up different stylistic registers. However, the place of her flower gathering during a moment of reflection, and also when we know she is under mortal threat from Queen Dionyza, makes Ophelia, who turns to flowers during her crisis, a suggestive comparison (*Hamlet* 4.5.180–6). The close connections between the four romances and the other late works can threaten to obscure links with earlier plays and give a false sense of a total schism in Shakespeare's career. But with this caveat in place, there is clearly a close connection with the other late plays here, and it is one that is arguably closer than anything in the first two acts of the play—though it remains intriguing that in some senses the first late Shakespearian moments are actually written by Wilkins.

The latter part of *Pericles* in a way dramatizes discovery partly by seeming in itself to be founded on a process of finding something new or something lost. It shows its explosive genesis in a storm, and then dramatizes the difficulty of the process of discovery again, in the powerful scene between Pericles and Marina, and maybe also in the magical revival of Thaisa. While it may not be productive to limit this fascinating text by seeing it only in terms of divided authorship or a dubious text, it is also not clearly better to see it as an even and/or entirely complete thing. The interaction between reader and text produces some interestingly uneven reactions: authorial intention (which is essentially unrecoverable) is not at issue here. What we have are illusions of intention, and illusions of explanations outside the play. *Pericles* is a play, a text, with peaks and troughs, and the peaks produce a dramatic intensity that escapes the confines of the plot, inviting readers and audiences to invent the stories that lie behind such moments. What also emerges is a distinct identity for 'late Shakespeare': this reading of *Pericles*, tempered though it is by various qualifications, strongly suggests that it is meaningful to discuss the separate agenda of Shakespeare's final works. It also offers the possibility that we can infer the author's own awareness of this new direction. This (as has been said) makes Shakespeare seem like a writer more explicitly involved in the shaping of his own literary career than is often thought.

The Tempest also tempts us to fill in a wider context in which the author meditates upon the end of something. The most fitting story is that of the author's retirement from the stage, or at least from writing plays on his own. However, it may contain notes of ending, but it is not the end. The mood of discovery and revelation that seems to come to life in *Pericles* continues through the romances and is there in *The Tempest*, but the later plays do not culminate or conclude the theme. Indeed, it grows in complexity. All four romances, and other late works, share this interest and a common formula in which to express it. Heavenly grace and the power of providence are felt acutely throughout, but Shakespeare does not in the end espouse them as simple, ultimate solutions.

Early in *The Tempest* there is a brief exchange between Prospero and Miranda during Prospero's narration of past events. Miranda asks, not unreasonably, why they did not drown in their fragile boat, and how they ended up on the island: 'How came we ashore?' (1.2.159). Her father gives an obvious reply: 'By providence divine' (1.2.160). It is less obvious what value to attribute to this, since it could operate as rather a platitude, or indeed as a profound statement of religious faith. When Ferdinand explains to his father how he came across Miranda, he says something similar: 'by immortal providence she's mine' (5.1.192). In any play providence has a curious status, as the idea of divine foreknowledge overlaps with the similar foreknowledge of the play's structure, and its author. So providence can create opportunities for irony, when it coincides with and highlights the design of the work and (especially in the case of *The Tempest*) the plans of characters. It would be wrong, however, to underestimate the seriousness of the idea in Shakespeare's time: it is a vital emphasis in Protestant theology that all events are predestined. Christianity has at its heart a faith in things to come, and providential stories give consolation in their representations of happy outcomes for those who suffer. Indeed, the dramatic representation of providential patterns may act as a strong reinforcement of the idea that the world is indeed governed by a benign force. However, alongside this positive idea of providence it is also important to recognize the particular inflection on the topic provided by Protestant theology. Calvin, for example, stressed the absoluteness and the inscrutability of predestination. While there was no prospect of doubting that things followed God's plan, or that this was a good plan, the structure of providence was completely beyond human comprehension. Any thought that fate could be influenced or properly understood was obliterated by the recognition of the absolute power of God. Whether Shakespeare's audience or Shakespeare himself were followers of Calvin's teaching or not, this stark notion of divine grace was powerfully present in the intellectual and spiritual life of the day.

So, while Shakespeare's romances are to some extent based on a positive providential structure, it is always worth remembering that this apparently benign way of seeing the world harboured some sharp and brutal possibilities. Their central figures find themselves in dire situations from which they are rescued by a variety of forces: time, gods, virtue, the growth of children, luck, magic, scheming, and other things that tend either to reflect or imitate the providential scheme. This is a perennial feature of romance, in which travails and eventual triumph are common features; it is a vital feature of Shakespearian romance because it is infused with extra energy. It is also something that features in many plays: it is very much at home in Shakespeare's constantly self-conscious drama, where the idea of a grand controlling structure is often at issue, and in question. The most intense engagement with providence is, perhaps, in *Hamlet*. The hero has a strong reason to believe in its power, as it offers a way past his own delay. Its appearance in the play, however, is complex and Hamlet himself seems to twitch nervously around the topic. At first glance his espousal of a providential theory of his exploits on the ship to England seems hearty and heartfelt:

> Rashly—
> And praised be rashness for it: let us know
> Our indiscretion sometime serves us well

> When our dear plots do pall, and that should teach us
> There's a divinity that shapes our ends,
> Rough-hew them how we will.
>
> (5.2.6–11)

Horatio replies 'That is most certain', which should give us pause. This is a play in which prompt conviction needs to be questioned. Hamlet appeals to providence in a story of exploits that seem to have little connection to the character who brooded in Denmark. Any problem Horatio might have in believing it is glossed over by the providential gesture. In *Hamlet* the whole idea is a kind of glossing over, a way of removing action from the individual—which is an opportune solution to the hero's dilemma. Hamlet returns to this opportune idea later in the same scene, when Horatio wonders if he wants to postpone the fateful fencing match with Laertes:

> Not a whit. We defy augury. There's a special providence in the fall of a sparrow. If it be now, 'tis not to come. If it be not to come, it will be now. If it be not now, yet it will come. The readiness is all. Since no man has aught of what he leaves, what is't to leave betimes?
>
> (5.2.165–70)

Hamlet bamboozles Horatio again with his quibbling over tenses and possible outcomes. The idea is superficially satisfactory but the play reveals it to be more superficial than satisfactory, a way of evading responsibility rather than a way of paying due respect to the Almighty. The philosophical temper of *Hamlet* is different from that of Shakespeare's late work: the earlier play is infused with scepticism and doubt, while the later plays have more at stake in a frank exploration of faith. Up to a point these plays, and indeed elements of other late works, can be seen as inspired by a passionate encounter with Christianity. This inspiration is questioned—the world of *Hamlet* is not far away—and while there are hints of a revelatory mood, there are also hints of irony around the patterns of thought that adhere to a providential drama. The irony does not destroy the energy and hope of the Christian revelation, but it enriches it in such a way as to provoke difficult questions.

The Winter's Tale offers a clear opportunity to map out a Christian scheme. The King sins in doubting his wife and in sending his legitimate daughter away to die on a foreign shore. This sin results in the death of his son, and the apparent death of his wife. After a period of fitting repentance things are restored to Leontes and he re-enters a state of grace. The courtier Cleomenes sums this up, but tellingly at a point before the action of providence has been revealed:

> Sir, you have done enough, and have performed
> A saint-like sorrow. No fault could you make
> Which you have not redeemed, indeed, paid down
> More penitence than done trespass. At the last
> Do as the heavens have done, forget your evil.
> With them, forgive yourself.
>
> (5.1.1–6)

Paulina reacts sharply to this when it leads to the suggestion that the King should marry again: 'There is none worthy | Respecting her that's gone' (34–5). In the long run we know she has a special interest in deflecting such thoughts. In its immediate context, though, her response reveals that Cleomenes uses the language of a Christian spiritual journey ('saint-like sorrow', 'redeemed', 'penitence', 'trespass', 'forgive') but without authority. Cleomenes cannot testify that the heavens have truly forgiven Leontes. In Calvin's theology only God can give grace and only God can understand the process; in *The Winter's Tale* Paulina seems to have some of that power.[13] Though this speech is premature, its way of thinking is not alien to the play, which ends with redemption and restoration. The only words spoken by the Queen when she reveals herself in the final scene incorporate Christian ideas within a partly pagan speech addressed to her daughter:

> You gods, look down,
> And from your sacred vials pour your graces
> Upon my daughter's head. —Tell me, mine own,
> Where hast thou been preserved? Where lived? How found
> Thy father's court? For thou shalt hear that I,
> Knowing by Paulina that the oracle
> Gave hope thou wast in being, have preserved
> Myself to see the issue.
>
> (5.3.122–9)

The key Christian element is the idea of grace, or 'graces', the word for God's favour, without which nobody can enter Heaven, and which occurs frequently in *The Winter's Tale*. This must have struck a chord with an early seventeenth-century audience, even though the rest of Hermione's speech is not Christian. She makes specific reference to Paulina's plan to keep her hidden, a piece of deception that draws attention to the role of contrivances, including artistic contrivances, which mimic providence in this play. Nevertheless, there is a degree of spiritual intensity about Hermione's wish for her daughter, and it takes a form that reappears throughout Shakespeare's late work, in that she sees graces falling from above, in this case poured down by the gods in 'vials'.

Pericles follows a similar path, though the hero's transgression is less clear. The hero goes through a lengthy period of abjection that intersects with religious ideas: his situation is purgatorial, and it is also penitent. Gower's narration of Pericles' plight after he is falsely informed of his daughter's death portrays him in deep mourning:

> And Pericles, in sorrow all devoured,
> With sighs shot through, and biggest tears o'ershow'red,
> Leaves Tarsus, and again embarks. He swears
> Never to wash his face nor cut his hairs.
> He puts on sack-cloth, and to sea. He bears
> A tempest which his mortal vessel tears,
> And yet he rides it out.
>
> (Scene 18, 25–31)

Pericles is a classical play and its world is pagan, but this does not prevent Christian imagery emerging. The hero's sackcloth clothing recalls 'sackcloth and ashes' mourning clothes. In a similar way, the image of a man courageously riding out the pains of his 'mortal vessel' is Christian in nature, especially when, as in *Pericles*, it leads to spiritual reward:

> O Helicanus, strike me, honoured sir,
> Give me a gash, put me to present pain,
> Lest this great sea of joys rushing upon me
> O'erbear the shores of my mortality
> And drown me with their sweetness!
>
> (Scene 21, 178–82)

This comes at the moment when Pericles realizes that Marina is his daughter. The shock of revelation is expressed in terms that are not singly Christian, but the onrush of joy has parallels in Christian imagery, as will be seen below. Pericles' 'joys', like Hermione's 'graces', come in liquid form, here in such intensity that they threaten to 'drown' the receiver.

This image of joys falling or rushing down has echoes throughout Shakespeare's late work, to the extent that they constitute a religious motif. In each of the romances the image occurs at a key point. In *Cymbeline* this comes when Belarius hands over the King's two sons:

> But, gracious sir,
> Here are your sons again, and I must lose
> Two of the sweet'st companions in the world.
> The benediction of these covering heavens
> Fall on their heads like dew, for they are worthy
> To inlay heaven with stars.
>
> (5.6.348–53)

Belarius bestows a pseudo-fatherly blessing by asking for heavenly grace to fall from above in a reversal of the situation in *The Winter's Tale* (where Hermione is receiving rather than returning her offspring). Again a character looks upwards and asks for a liquid benediction: here 'dew' is to carry grace onto the boys' heads. In *The Tempest*, when Prospero overlooks Ferdinand and Miranda declaring love for one another, he looks to a heavenly rain: 'Fair encounter | Of two most rare affections! Heavens rain grace | On that which breeds between 'em!' (3.1.74–6).[14] Ferdinand and Miranda are actually given such a blessing twice. The second is Gonzalo's, at the end of the play:

> I have inly wept,
> Or should have spoke ere this. Look down, you gods,
> And on this couple drop a blessèd crown,
> For it is you that have chalked forth the way
> Which brought us hither.
>
> (5.1.203–7)

Alonso endorses this wish—'I say amen, Gonzalo' (5.1.207)—but we may discern a note of genial mockery as he gives affectionate credit to his sentimental friend. This small note of irony, however, does not detract from this as part of a recurring religious motif. At key points in all the four romances characters imagine themselves or the younger generation receiving grace in a passionate spiritual moment. In each case a different way is found of imagining this grace being sent down by God, or the gods, from above, as a crown, a sea, rain, dew, or the liquid from 'sacred vials'. The temptation is to link these up in a biographical story, and to link them with a great spiritual experience on the part of the author. The plays could reflect this moment of religious conversion with reverberating moments of theatrical intensity. However, this requires yet another fictionalization of Shakespeare's life, and indeed one may simply reverse the formula: this motif is a way of reflecting a repeated moment of theatrical intensity with the imagery of religious conversion.

These mainstream moments, where the spiritual intensity is in tune with the dynamics of the romance plot, are not the whole story, and a fuller understanding of their value only comes when further reverberations of the grace-from-above theme are traced elsewhere. The first echo comes in *Henry VIII*, when Queen Katherine, facing death, expresses her wishes for her daughter:

> In which I have commended to his goodness
> The model of our chaste loves, his young daughter—
> The dews of heaven fall thick in blessings on her—
> Beseeching him to give her virtuous breeding.
> She is young, and of a noble modest nature.
> I hope she will deserve well—and a little
> To love her for her mother's sake, that loved him,
> Heaven knows how dearly.

> (4.2.132–9)

The facts of past history interfere with the romance tone. Shakespeare's audience might well have in mind that Katherine's daughter Mary does not turn out to 'deserve well', at least in the mind of a Protestant audience, as she becomes a Catholic Queen. So while the motif of blessings falling as a heavenly dew is exactly in tune with the mood of other late plays, its full meaning in context is not. There is a slightly less discordant but nevertheless problematic appearance of the idea in *The Two Noble Kinsmen*:

> His part is played, and, though it were too short,
> He did it well. Your day is lengthened and
> The blissful dew of heaven does arrouse you.
> The powerful Venus well hath graced her altar,
> And given you your love.

> (5.6.102–6)

The Quarto text has 'arowze' in line 104; 'arrouse' means 'to sprinkle, fall gently upon' and derives from the Latin *ros* (dew), which makes it doubly appropriate. Here again it is more or less in tune, as Palamon is rewarded for his faithful love by receiving Emilia, but Palamon has won his love after losing a battle, and was saved from death only by the bizarre death of his cousin and friend (and sworn enemy) Arcite. So he is 'arroused' by this 'blissful dew', but this is hardly an unambiguous moment of faith and hope. Evidently there are problems with the grace-from-above motif in Shakespeare's late work, and this needs to be taken into account when exploring the reasons for the persistence of such a theme. Before looking at further echoes, and further problems, it is necessary to establish some context for this idea outside Shakespeare's work.

The most important source for such Christian imagery is naturally the Bible. The idea of heavenly dew as a form of blessing appears in the Old Testament first in Exodus, where the Israelites in the desert encounter manna. It appears 'when the dew that was fallen was ascended': 'a small round thing was upon the face of the wilderness, small as the hoar frost on the earth' (Exodus 16: 14).[15] So this heavenly gift of food appears like a kind of dew or frost. In the Book of Deuteronomy the theme appears in a prophetic context and strikes a tone perhaps closer to the prayers of characters in Shakespeare's romances: 'Israel the fountain of Jacob shall dwell alone in safety in a land of wheat and wine; and his heavens shall drop down the dew' (Deuteronomy 33: 28). This promises a better life after one full of care, with the dew as a symbol of God's bounty. In the Psalms there is another image recognizable from the romances, heavenly rain, this time used in praise of God's generosity to the world as it is:

Thou visitest the earth, and waterest it: thou makest it very rich: the River of God is full of water: thou preparest them corn: for so thou appointest it. Thou waterest abundantly the furrows thereof: thou causest the rain to descend into the valleys thereof: thou makest it soft with showers, and blessest the bud thereof.   (Psalm 65: 9–10).

In the New Testament two key episodes see a communication between earth and heaven falling from above. One is when the Holy Spirit descends at Jesus' baptism: 'And Jesus when he was baptized, came straight out of the water. And lo, the heavens were opened unto him, and John saw the Spirit of God, descending like a dove, and lighting upon him' (Matthew 3: 16). Baptism itself is recalled by the falling liquids of Shakespeare's romances, as characters are in effect born again into new hope. Another biblical forerunner comes on the day of Pentecost: 'And suddenly there came a sound from heaven, as of a rushing and mighty wind, and it filled all the house where they sat. And there appeared unto them cloven tongues, like fire, and it sat upon each of them' (Acts 2: 2–3). In both cases the Holy Spirit comes down from heaven and fills those below. Although the dove, the fire, and the wind are very different from the liquid graces of Shakespeare's romances, there is surely a pattern here which feeds into the religious mood of his plays—a physical pattern, of things falling from above, and a spiritual pattern, in which people are inspired and blessed by divine forces.

The grace-from-above motif appears, not surprisingly, in devotional poetry of the period. John Davies of Hereford, writing at exactly the time of the late romances, provides a good example of the suggestiveness of such an image. He wrote on various subjects, including religion, and moved in some of the same circles as Shakespeare—he was certainly acquainted with Fletcher, for example. His 1609 poem *The Holy Roode* extemporizes on the theme of 'the dew of Grace':

> This dew of grace ne'er fails but straight the sun
> Of justice doth exhale it to his sphere;
> And if the foulest face it over-run,
> In mercy's eyes it makes it crystal clear.
>> For eyes that so o'erflow, are wells of grace,
>> Wherein God loves to look, to see his face![16]

The association of this dew with tears is striking because it resonates with the key instances of the idea in Shakespeare. For Hermione, Belarius, and Queen Katherine, tears are surely appropriate and each asks for heaven to match these tears with its own. Though Gonzalo asks for a crown to drop on Miranda and Ferdinand, he says he 'inly wept' before speaking. Pericles represents the most concrete connection: the 'sea' that threatens to drown him in its 'sweetness' can be a sea of tears, or a sea of heavenly grace. Both Shakespeare and Davies explore how tears may be a way of imagining the arrival of grace at a moment of great joy. Davies echoes the Shakespearian motif again in his 1612 poem 'A Confession of a Sinner', where he asks the Lord to 'pour ... thy precious balms of grace' (59) into his heart.[17] The power of his spiritual pain is present in Shakespeare's romances, and they both imagine a similar solution. Recent critics have become very exercised by the possibility that Shakespeare was a Catholic, and so it is of some relevance that Davies probably was.[18] It seems likely at least, and not surprising given the short timescale of the Reformation, that Shakespeare had sympathy of some kind (a memory, a tendency, or an allegiance) to Catholic imagery or practices. The particular image being discussed here, however, is better seen as a more generally Christian topos that has become deeply bound up with and embedded in a set of interests that do not derive from any particular religious affiliation.

The motif of grace-from-above in Shakespeare, and in particular its liquid properties, clearly has substantial connections with Christian writing, both in the Bible and in devotional works. So one can begin to associate the tone of these late romances more specifically with religious experiences such as revelation, conversion, and redemption. Before pursuing this idea fully, however, one has to account for further appearances of the idea. There is a problematic group of three instances surrounding Cardinal Wolsey in *Henry VIII*. The first is an aside, and relatively innocent:

> For it is you
> Have blown this coal betwixt my lord and me,
> Which God's dew quench. Therefore I say again,
> I utterly abhor, yea, from my soul,
> Refuse you for my judge, whom yet once more
> I hold my most malicious foe, and think not
> At all a friend to truth.

> (2.4.76–82)

Queen Katherine attacks the scheming Cardinal for engineering her rift with the King, and hopes that the resultant fire will be quenched by 'God's dew'. The idea receives a faint echo here, one that does not necessarily separate itself from conventional devout statements—although it does add to the overall presence of the motif. More awkward are two allusions to it in a very different context, when Wolsey defends himself against the King's anger:

> My sovereign, I confess your royal graces
> Showered on me daily have been more than could

> My studied purposes requite ...
>   For your great graces
> Heaped upon me, poor undeserver, I
> Can nothing render but allegiant thanks.

(3.2.167–9, 175–7)

The many nuances of grace create an odd echo here, as Wolsey's words clearly connect with the patterns discussed above, although he is talking about money and temporal preferment, and not spiritual salvation. Likewise the idea of being 'showered' is almost a travesty of the devout wish for a divine soaking that linked Pericles, Hermione, and Belarius. Remarkably, Henry picks up the image from Wolsey and turns it back on him:

>   I presume
> That as my hand has opened bounty to you,
> My heart dropped love, my power rained honour, more
> On you than any ...

(3.2.184–7)

The King's reference to his 'power' that 'rained honour' comes third, as if he had to work himself up to emulating his subject's high-flown imagery. But here it is imagery in a simple sense, rather than a numinous statement that can be linked with powerful religious themes. In *Henry VIII*, then, the motif established at key moments in the romances, and also at a sharp-edged moment in the very same play, multiplies and begins to lose its focus.

The same process is evident in *The Tempest*, where two more echoes remove the motif from the spiritual realm. The first comes in the masque Prospero puts on for Miranda and Ferdinand. The goddess Ceres hails Iris the 'many-coloured messenger' and praises the 'honey-drops, refreshing showers' that she 'diffusest' on her flowers (4.1.76–9). Although there is no bathos here, as there is still a high-flown context, there is a relative inertia to the religious force of the idea, as Ceres and Iris are classical deities fully encased within their masque, unable to speak actively or directly to a wider religious realm. Caliban gives a more challenging variation on the theme in a passage also discussed in the previous chapter:

> Sometimes a thousand twangling instruments
> Will hum about mine ears, and sometime voices

That if I then had waked after long sleep
Will make me sleep again; and then in dreaming
The clouds methought would open and show riches
Ready to drop upon me, that when I waked
I cried to dream again.

(3.2.140–6)

Characters in the romances encounter the strange, dreamlike reality of their happy endings; for them the amazing thing is that heaven's grace is truly falling upon them. Caliban can only find such intensity within his unshared dream, but he too imagines riches falling from clouds just like rain. Up to a point this corroborates the feeling in *The Tempest* and in the other romances that one might connect their providential structures with an intense Christian faith and hope. However, the fact that it is private, unreal, ultimately thwarted, and not sanctioned by the power structures within the play makes Caliban's version of the motif poignant in a troubling way. At the very least, it is a reverberation of the idea of grace-from-above that tends against a clear interpretation.

The Winter's Tale poses a challenge to its characters and audiences and readers in that they must find ways of understanding what has happened. How, for example, are they to reconcile the role of providence with the role of contrivance? One character, Autolycus, has a kind of radical solution to this problem that leads him towards two awkward echoes of the grace-from-above motif. He encounters everything as the work of chance, and all things are therefore opportunities in waiting. He says, 'If I had a mind to be honest, I see fortune would not suffer me. She drops booties in my mouth' (4.4.832–3); and later, 'Now, had I not the dash of my former life in me, would preferment drop on my head' (5.2.112–13). In his mind the 'dew of Grace' becomes mere pennies from heaven. It is difficult to know whether to take Autolycus as a reflection back on the heart of the play, in that we see his limited understanding translate its marvels into the banal trappings of luck, or to see him as a vital ironist, refusing to participate in an artificial exemplification of providence. What is worth emphasizing is that this final and most travestied variation on the revelatory theme does not remove its value. For one could argue that the presence of the motif in unexpected places and peculiar forms is eloquent testimony to the power of the idea. Its strength makes it echo in strange places; it moves in mysterious ways. The clearer point to make is that Shakespeare engages with a great spiritual potential in romance, and the plays incorporate echoes of religious conversion that parallel the redemptive quality inherent in the plot. However, Shakespeare does not allow the grace-from-above to go unexamined: it travels deeper into the structures of the texts and finds itself twisted and turned.

4

Family Romances

The late plays focus with unusual intensity on certain family dynamics, especially the relationship between father and daughter. They also focus on the fundamental importance of these bonds and on the healing power they have when they are restored after long separations. In Shakespeare's tragedies the same bond (as in *Romeo and Juliet*, *King Lear*, *Hamlet*, and *Othello*) features, in combination with the powerful pressure of the absent or present mother on her children. They are at the heart of the psychological dramas most of all because violent tragic power results from the dissolution of these bonds under extreme pressure. In Shakespeare's comedies fathers and daughters are again central, but the dynamic is very different. Daughters free themselves from their fathers' control and the comic ending is a celebration of a new domestic hierarchy, with them now closer to their new husbands than to their fathers. In the late plays the reunion of father and daughter (in *Cymbeline*, *The Winter's Tale*, and *Pericles*), the birth of a daughter (*Henry VIII*), or in the rather different case of *The Tempest*, the comic transference of the daughter from father to husband, but under strict paternal control, are all vital to the emotional structures of the plays. Accordingly, critics such as Cyrus Hoy, interested in the 'psychological climate which produces the romances', emphasize the positive nature of this relationship: 'The dramatist is engaged in a quest to free the imagination from all the shrill mistress-wife-mother figures who have inhabited the late tragedies, and to create in their place an ideal of femininity on whom the imagination can bestow its tenderest sentiments, without the distraction of sexual desire.'[1] While this may work as a broad summary, the imaginative and emotional energy of these plays is not so well ordered. This chapter will explore moments where sexual desire turns out to be a distraction that the plays find it rather hard to resist, and guilt sometimes impinges on purer emotions. It is perhaps complacent to argue that having daughters as the idealized feminine figures will preclude sexual desire, and it will prove troubling and dangerous if it does surface. These plays do indeed, in the end, propose a tender and cherishing form of love based in the comfort and purity of family bonds, but this is still subject to the trials and tribulations of a corrupt world. Shakespeare is too subtle to allow familial love to blossom without any complications.

In *Pericles* the daughter-heroine Marina is pure to a comical extent as she pursues her strange career as a virgin prostitute who converts her clients to moral lives. When she meets Pericles, the purity she has to offer almost completely overcomes any anxieties that might attend a scene where a father visits his beautiful unknown daughter, recently freed from a brothel, for comfort. However, this episodic play starts with incest—this is the original sin of the play that starts the prince's wanderings. The play's structure juxtaposes beginning and end in a forceful contrast. Pericles is redeemed from the original sin, but the fact that it was not his original sin, nor everybody's, is an imbalance in the equation. Furthermore, it is possible to argue that the juxtaposition might create affinity as well as contrast—binary oppositions are not always stable. There is considerable virtue in Richard McCabe's analysis of incest in Shakespearian romance: 'Whereas tragic incest unleashes the destructive forces of nature, its "romantic" counterpart endeavours resolution through a sublimation of forbidden desire, an assumption of the temporal and profane into the eternal and sacred frequently symbolized by the intervention of some *deus ex machina*.'[2] For McCabe, romance turns towards the supernatural, on which scale incestuous energy can be redefined and accommodated within a heightened atmosphere and correspondingly intense relationships. This provides a template that can be considered throughout this chapter. The numerous signs of discordant passion may perhaps be part of the play's tendency towards a new and bolder vision of reality. However, this should not be allowed to blunt the sharpness of these moments.

One problem with the play's beginning is the riddle with which Antiochus tests his daughter's suitors. Pericles realizes the truth but then does not know what to do. It seems mortally dangerous to show that he has guessed the secret, mortally dangerous to pretend failure and face the consequences. Most intriguing of all is that Antiochus is impressed that Pericles has worked out the answer. The riddle itself is surely very simple:

> I am no viper, yet I feed
> On mother's flesh which did me breed.
> I sought a husband, in which labour
> I found that kindness in a father.
> He's father, son, and husband mild;
> I mother, wife, and yet his child.
> How this may be and yet in two,
> As you will live resolve it you.

(Scene 1, 107–14)

The third and fourth lines here are barely a riddle at all: only the slightest slippage of meaning in 'labour' and 'kindness' stops it being a plain and direct statement. The rest of the riddle is hardly more obscure. This makes the world of the play's first episode seem all the more alarming, a place where incest proclaims itself and everyone looks the other way. The situation is actually more complex, as within the play Pericles too finds no problem with the idea that he is the first to answer the riddle—so the tendency to ignore the obvious is central, and more pressing. Coppélia Kahn discusses the riddle in an essay in the tradition of psychoanalytic criticism: 'Riddles occur at points of life crisis in folklore and literature because the riddle structure offers an expressive model for the reconciliation of essential dualities. It creates confusion and then establishes clarity, reaffirming the rules and essential distinctions on which social life depends.'[3] Kahn also points out that behind this riddle lies the mythical *uroboros*, a snake that swallows its own tail, which she takes to be an image of the Oedipal family, doomed to repeat its destructive cycle. In Kahn's view, Pericles must be trapped in such a cycle, from which only the purity of his daughter, and his recognition of the value of their bond, can release him. Later in this chapter there will be more opportunity to consider how psychoanalytic interpretation may inform us about late Shakespeare. For now it is worth saying that this account of the play struggles with Thaisa, whose death is the true cause of Pericles' despair, rather than the incest riddle. The romances, after all, are about wives as well as daughters. In addition, this Oedipal map of *Pericles* does not capture the complex interactions of the various episodes. Its causal sequence does not fit with the play's less clear progress.

The final scene of reunion provides a different qualification of Cyrus Hoy's picture of 'pure affection'. The recognition scene between Pericles and Marina (Scene 21) is remarkably vivid and candid in both rhetoric and emotion. Even here, however, hints of buried incestuous innuendo emerge. When Pericles arrives in Mytilene he is in an abject, uncommunicative state, traumatized by the supposed deaths of wife and child. As has been mentioned, the first encounter with his daughter is in a strange context:

> LORD   Sir, we have a maid in Mytilene I durst wager
>   Would win some words of him.
> LYSIMACHUS   'Tis well bethought.
>   She questionless, with her sweet harmony
>   And other choice attractions, would alarum
>   And make a batt'ry through his deafened ports,
>   Which now are midway stopped.
>
> (Scene 21, 33-8)

The qualities in Marina that they hope to recruit are not sexual, but the mention of 'choice attractions' and the image of making 'a batt'ry through his deafened ports' run the risk of veering in that direction. Mytilene is a land of innuendo as well as a place of reformation and reunion, and the two modes come into difficult contact here. The lines quoted above are not innuendo: they are more like innuendo about innuendo. Shakespeare allows the words to imply that they might be implying something. It is a crucial distinction, but the curious charge attending this reunion does signify.

Recognitions operate on many levels: to recover a lost daughter can entail a partial recovery of a lost wife. In *The Winter's Tale* and in *Pericles* the issue of resemblance between wife and daughter, and the possibility of physical attraction that this might lead to, do appear. As above, the identification is made in essential innocence but the play also elicits other possibilities:

> My dearest wife was like this maid, and such
> My daughter might have been. My queen's square brows,
> Her stature to an inch, as wand-like straight,
> As silver-voiced, her eyes as jewel-like,
> And cased as richly, in pace another Juno,

Who starves the ears she feeds, and makes them hungry
The more she gives them speech.

(Scene 21, 96–102)

Pericles describes the physical qualities of his wife as they are recalled
in the appearance of the girl in front of him. His praise does not imply
a physical attraction, but there may be circumstances in which one
could reflect on the fact that what attracted once could attract again.
This description of unsatisfied appetites recalls amatory imagery in
general, and Enobarbus's description of Cleopatra specifically ('Other
women cloy | The appetites they feed, but she makes hungry | Where
most she satisfies', 2.2.242–4). In the end, however, the pressure
towards a sharp-edged sexual interpretation of the father–daughter
encounter is insufficient and these hints make up, instead, part of the
candid, passionate intensity of the reunion.

In *The Winter's Tale*, however, this undercurrent in the equivalent
reunion is stronger. Leontes' erotic life has been suspended after the
supposed death of Hermione, but things are progressing towards its
eventual continuation. Even Paulina, guardian of his wife's memory,
participates in the belief that he will marry again, though she knows
that he is, in fact, still married. In contrast, Pericles without Thaisa
has abandoned this side of life altogether. So it is a relatively vigorous
Leontes whose memory is stirred by Perdita. He is less vigorous,
however, than the central character in Robert Greene's *Pandosto*, the
main source of *The Winter's Tale*, who really does desire (unwittingly,
at the time) his daughter. This incestuous attraction is one of the
things weighing on Pandosto's conscience as he commits suicide.
Shakespeare defuses this and in his version Hermione is not dead for
good: there is no causal sequence between these two things, exactly,
but they are closely connected. Nevertheless in *The Winter's Tale* there
are moments when the incestuous energy surfaces briefly. There is a
sticky exchange at the end of the scene where Leontes meets Perdita
(as yet unidentified). Florizel, the son of his old friend Polixenes and
Perdita's intended, makes a courtly (and untrue) boast that his father
will grant Leontes precious things as if they were trifles. Leontes
replies:

LEONTES   Would he do so, I'd beg your precious mistress,
    Which he counts but a trifle.

PAULINA   Sir, my liege,
  Your eye hath too much youth in't. Not a month
  Fore your queen died she was more worth such gazes
  Than what you look on now.
LEONTES   I thought of her
  Even in these looks I made.

                                                    (5.1.222–7)

There may be a telling ambiguity in Leontes' statement that he was
thinking of his wife. This recognition, an intuition of the happy truth,
implies a transference of affection which unavoidably has a sexual
component. The King's words assuage Paulina, who interprets them
to mean that he has not forgotten his loyalty to Hermione and to
his bargain with her friend. However, there is more to them than
that. Leontes' reply to Florizel that sets Paulina off in the first place
is itself oddly out of place. The penitent King is briefly transformed
into a lecherous old man. The source intrudes briefly, perhaps; or the
complexity of love intrudes, making it difficult to feel secure about the
romance conclusion as it develops. Shakespeare creates recognition
scenes of extraordinary intensity, and one ingredient of this intensity
is an erotic frisson.

Subtexts and ambiguities can reveal sharp truths and untruths.
Odd moments in the plays can reveal faultlines in their fabric. One
such moment is when Leontes reacts so suddenly and extremely in
suspecting his wife of adultery. Explanations range from contemporary
or modern ideas about psychology to simple dramatic ineptitude.[4] It
is useful to consider Leontes' sudden passion alongside a later point in
the play, when his erstwhile friend Polixenes (who has been wrongly
suspected of adultery with Leontes' wife) rails against Perdita and
Florizel:

                              And you, enchantment,
          Worthy enough a herdsman—yea, him too,
          That makes himself, but for our honour therein,
          Unworthy thee—if ever henceforth thou
          These rural latches to his entrance open,
          Or hoop his body more with thy embraces,
          I will devise a death as cruel for thee
          As thou art tender to't.

                                                    (4.4.434–41)

Polixenes' passionate intensity recalls that of Leontes in the first scene. The strength of his language is all the more incongruous given the pastoral setting into which it intrudes. It raises the question as to what leads to this disproportionate intensity. There is spare energy, sometimes spare sexual energy, sometimes more generalized energy but around sexual contexts, in the romances. It does not exactly undermine the spiritual nature of the reunions and family groupings of the ends of the plays, but it demonstrates the chaos against which such positive images have to exist.

A similar incongruous intensity occurs in *The Tempest*, when Prospero achieves what seems like a surprising level of anger against Ferdinand. The young man's crime is to fall in love with Miranda. The father's tetchiness about this sits strangely at times with the fact that it all fits with his grand plan:

> (*Aside*) They are both in either's powers. But this swift business
> I must uneasy make, lest too light winning
> Make the prize light. (*To Ferdinand*) One word more. I charge thee
> That thou attend me. Thou dost here usurp
> The name thou ow'st not; and hast put thyself
> Upon this island as a spy, to win it
> From me the lord on't.

(1.2.453–9)

Prospero goes on to sentence Ferdinand to a brisk session of manacles, sea-water, roots, and mussels—a session of being Caliban, which offers some awkward parallels given Caliban's reported attempt to rape Miranda. Prospero speaks aside to the audience here, saying that his purpose is to ensure that the 'prize' is not too 'light'. We could therefore interpret his hasty claim that Ferdinand has designs on the island as a cunning smokescreen so Ferdinand will not realize why he is being tested. Caliban also wanted, and still wants, to rule the island, and his assault on Miranda had a dynastic and territorial motive. He and Ferdinand parallel one another in various respects, and both attract the wrath of Prospero: the belief that his charges against Ferdinand are invented with a benign aim comes under pressure from their closeness to those against Caliban. Those against Caliban also look different, now less secure given Prospero's willingness to contrive accusations against another suitor. In addition to this, Prospero does not seem entirely in control. Instead of the effortless illusions perpetrated on the other shipwrecked characters at the beginning of the play, there is strain and rage. So Prospero's aside here fails to explain adequately the compulsion to make the lovers 'uneasy'.

The strain on Prospero grows as the play continues, though ultimately he relinquishes rage. Anyone reading this psychologically might come to the conclusion that the key usurpation effected by Ferdinand puts him between Prospero and his daughter. Later in the play the Duke shows an interest in his daughter's chastity that is outside the usual parameters of paternal concern:

> But
> If thou dost break her virgin-knot before
> All sanctimonious ceremonies may
> With full and holy rite be ministered,
> No sweet aspersion shall the heavens let fall
> To make this contrast grow; but barren hate,
> Sour-eyed disdain, and discord, shall bestrew
> The union of your bed with weeds so loathly
> That you shall hate it both.
>
> (4.1.14–22)

The lack of a 'sweet aspersion' would deprive the lovers of a key motif in the late plays: the falling of grace from above. The problem here, perhaps, is that the sanctity of marriage is expressed in terms which are to some extent metonymic, but do not quite clearly stay metonymic. Marriage is represented by a part of itself, the bed, but the bed seems uncomfortably literal and the sexual component is prominent—as if this is where Prospero's thoughts remain. This could all be explained in terms of political advantage. Miranda is a key bargaining tool in her father's rapprochement with the King of Naples, Ferdinand's father, and her stock is higher if she is a virgin. However, the fact that we need to explain it away tells us something—it tells us that this does not read like proportionate parental concern.

Leontes' paranoid passion has the characteristics of a horrific dream. This analogy makes the natural connection between the hidden horrors that seem to underlie the strange, dark hints in these plays, and psychoanalysis, which in its analyses of desires and repressions offers suggestive models of how different levels of activity intersect and interfere. A psychoanalytic approach can offer nuanced responses to texts, though its application is always complex. It might focus on one (or more) different areas: on the content of the work, especially its characters; on the author; on the form of the work; or on the reader (perhaps conceived very generally, as a representative of a wider culture). The first two—characters and authors—may be problematic in straightforward ways: psychoanalysis is an interactive process, and it is strange to aim it at an unresponding or unrecoverable author, or at a character whose fragmentary, textual nature means that anything truly analysable must be inferred or invented. Nevertheless it is a common and understandable habit of reading to infer psychologies for characters and authors from the evidence found in texts, and accordingly this approach has been evident in some suggestive criticism of the late plays. David Sundelson, for example, sees the central father figure in the romances exerting an obsessive control over his daughter.[5] Coppélia Kahn, on the other hand, sees reunion in *Pericles* heralding a development in the central character: 'through her [Marina] Pericles becomes a father anew, accepting his fatherhood as his identity, and stops trying vainly to deny his mortality'.[6] The plots of other rulers—Cymbeline, Leontes, Prospero, and perhaps Henry VIII—could be interpreted in the same way: the central characters are reconciled to their own mortality by embracing the existence and growth of the next generation.

Since Freud psychoanalysts have been deeply interested in dreams, so it is not surprising that when characters dream they find critics to analyse them. Caliban's dream in *The Tempest* is seen to feature an image of the lost maternal breast, while Jupiter in Posthumus's dream thinly veils his true identity as the hero's dead father. Janet Adelman's book *Suffocating Mothers* looks at maternal origins. For her the final phase of Shakespeare's negotiation with mother-figures sees a kind of purgation which is in some cases restorative. This book is interesting because it moves away from psychoanalysing characters, and turns to Shakespeare himself: 'The repeated cycle of doing and undoing—*Pericles* to *Cymbeline*, *The Winter's Tale* to *The Tempest*—suggests the deep divisions in Shakespeare's psychic world: even at the end, he cannot fully join together what he has put asunder in *Hamlet*.'[7] While this is a strong and intriguing way of reading a text, one might argue that it cannot read an author fully, since the text is the only evidence available. The more esoteric possibilities of psychoanalytic criticism—analysing the form of the work, or the reader—might actually offer the possibility of achieving something more concrete in relation to the measurable experience of reading the text. While the author is in some ways a far more solid basis for enquiry, in practice the evidence available yields relatively intangible results. If one focuses on the form of the work, the fascinating possibility emerges that one might be able to read, between the lines of the text, not a character's or author's subconscious, but the virtual subconscious of the play itself—the hidden desires of genre (destructive hints in comedy), or the covert difficulties of an individual play in becoming itself, and achieving its aim. Alternatively, the resistance or inhibition or discordant emotion might be inferred not in form but in the reader's apprehension of the work. The text, in this model, elicits conflicting and complex responses in the reader that are analogous to a conscious and unconscious encounter with its features. All this may seem abstruse but in Shakespearian romance the actual source of the complex, strange elements is by nature difficult to pin down. The ways in which, say, the happy reunion of father and daughter in *The Winter's Tale* might evoke some out-of-place dynamics are more fully understood if the inferred psychological processes are not only those of the characters.

With this multifaceted possibility in psychoanalytic criticism in mind, it becomes possible to see varied nuances in another repeated story or motif in the late plays. These relate to the invocation of childhood—memories of unusual vividness and intensity occur at a number of places in the romances. These are ripe material for psychoanalysis, but they need not only illuminate the problems of individual characters. Rather they are sharp edges of the grand family-based structures of these plays. The classic example is that of Leontes and Polixenes in *The Winter's Tale*. In the first scene Camillo describes how the two Kings were close friends as children:

> Sicilia cannot show himself over-kind to Bohemia. They were trained together in their childhoods; and there rooted betwixt them then such an affection which cannot choose but branch now. Since their more mature dignities and royal necessities made separation of their society, their encounters—though not personal—hath been royally attorneyed with interchange of gifts, letters, loving embassies, that they have seemed to be together, though absent; shook hands as over a vast; and embraced as it were from the ends of opposed winds. The heavens continue their loves.

(1.1.21–32)

This scene is based in two kinds of convention: that of courtly formality, where two lords exchange pleasantries without really telling one another anything, and that of dramatic introduction, where minor figures set up a scene. But there are imbalances here. One is that the Bohemian lord is one Archidamus, who never speaks again in the play. The Sicilian lord, however, is Camillo, close confidant of Leontes and subsequently of Polixenes. He, not Hermione, is the person who really does leave Leontes for a new man. In keeping with this, Camillo's information is more intimate than we might expect. He starts with a neat little analogy that describes the two Kings' friendships like two plants growing together, and then naturally following different paths. But in the description of these two men seeming to be together, though absent, a different register of affection seems to be introduced—these are the attributes of lovers.

The seed planted by this grows when the Kings themselves return to the theme. Polixenes describes an idealized shared childhood at a critical point in the play, when Hermione is persuading him to stay in Sicilia. It immediately precedes Leontes' 'Too hot, too hot!' outburst as he suddenly interprets all her courtly persuasion as a sign of infidelity. Hermione questions Polixenes quite playfully about what sort of boys her husband and his friend were. The reply, I think, has a rather different tone from the question 'was not my lord the verier wag o'th' two?':

> We were as twinned lambs that did frisk i'th' sun,
> And bleat the one at th'other. What we changed
> Was innocence for innocence. We knew not
> The doctrine of ill-doing, nor dreamed
> That any did. Had we pursued that life,
> And our weak spirits ne'er been higher reared
> With stronger blood, we should have answered heaven
> Boldly, 'Not guilty'.

(1.2.69–76)

Polixenes imagines this idyll as real, and the world of sin and experience as a dream, but to us it seems the other way round. It is a strange thing to say to the woman who is blamed for ending this innocence, and a strange thing anyway to speak so candidly about this anxiety. The speed with which the two Kings slip into rages might be connected with their strained initiations into the world of experience, but I would prefer not to link things up into a causal chain. Instead, these various moments of tonal inconsistency and tangential intensity are a rich part of the play's effect, adding texture to the structure of romance.

Marjorie Garber discusses this childhood friendship in her book *Coming of Age in Shakespeare*.[8] The nostalgic look back to an innocent time makes the path to adulthood look like a fall from grace. It looks all the more like one when, in retrospect, childhood was a time of simple certainties. Garber argues that nostalgia for the lost 'twin' inhibits the necessary process of individuation. From another angle, the struggle to become an individual is evaded by recourse to an old source of shared identity and comfort: Leontes in particular is unable to function within new relationships because of the legacy of his first, innocent love. J. I. M. Stewart also looks at this relationship in his earlier book *Character and Motive in Shakespeare*.[9] He sees it as the root of Leontes' jealousy. The King, for Stewart, is affected by a deep-buried attachment to Polixenes—Stewart thinks it distinctly homosexual, but it could be a more general, misguided attachment to innocent days. The jealousy surfaces under the stimulus of socially sanctioned flirtation which in this case takes a destructive turn. Only someone troubled by something else—as Stewart says Leontes is—fails to understand the codes of normal behaviour and misreads them so drastically.

In *The Two Noble Kinsmen* there are three friendships in central positions, and these too show moments of distracting intensity. It is worth also saying that friendship and intensity are themes visited in earlier plays too. In the final chapter I shall contrast the treatment of the theme in *The Two Gentlemen of Verona* and *The Two Noble Kinsmen*. Another play of great interest is *A Midsummer Night's Dream*, where the close friendship of Hermia and Helena in their childhoods is a precedent for that of Emilia and Flavina—and there is the additional parallel between the plays in question, which is that Theseus and Hippolyta (derived from Chaucer's *Knight's Tale*) are monarchs of both. The friendship between Hermia and Helena becomes a focus of tension in their love stories, but it does not inhibit their erotic progress in the same manifest way it does in the later plays. The repetition of topoi in plays written in chronological contiguity and with a plethora of common dynamics is significant, and perhaps all the more so because it intersects with longer-held interests. So it is important that there are more friendships, and interestingly different ones. In *Pericles* the young Marina grows up in the foster care of King Creon. He has a daughter of similar age who compares unfavourably with Marina in every respect:

> our Cleon has
> One daughter, and a full-grown lass
> E'en ripe for marriage-rite. This maid
> Hight Philoten, and it is said
> For certain in our story she
> Would ever with Marina be,
> Be't when they weaved the sleided silk
> With fingers long, small, white as milk;
> Or when she would with sharp nee'le wound
> The cambric which she made more sound
> By hurting it, or when to th' lute
> She sung, and made the night bird mute,
> That still records with moan; or when
> She would with rich and constant pen
> Vail to her mistress Dian. Still
> This Philoten contends in skill
> With absolute Marina; so
> With the dove of Paphos might the crow
> Vie feathers white.

(Scene 15, 15–33)

This causes understandable tension, and Cleon's wife Dionyza conceives murderous wishes—the bracing, candid style of the Chorus Gower delivers the details in a brisk sequence. This childhood association between two girls does not develop into innocent mutuality. The other examples where something more pure and perfect results all precede the action of the plays in question, by some distance: embroiled in time and the sequence of action, things go wrong. The innocent ways in which Marina shows her prowess all have problematic subtexts. The needle wounding the cambric seems like a figure for the loss of virginity, and yet the cloth survives, 'more sound': very fitting for a character whose career as a prostitute will spread purity. The competition with the 'night bird' is revealing because if this is the nightingale, as seems very likely (the *Oxford English Dictionary* records the word used to refer to other birds as well, but none so noted for its singing), then it invokes the myth of Philomel, in which the heroine is raped and then transformed. This story is already haunting

Pericles in the name of Cleon's daughter. To add to this confusion, the original quarto text has the words 'night bed' instead of 'night bird'. We owe 'night bird', which is surely right, to a later editor, but the ghost of 'night bed' in the Quarto provides a sexual undertone.[10] Pursuing this reading leads to the 'moan' of this 'night bed', a sexual sound that Marina makes 'mute'. Pursuing such a reading also leads the critic towards an intriguing kind of prurience: sex is definitely not going on here, but the act of reading closely can discover, or perhaps provide (pictures of innocence held up to view can find themselves compromised) an erotic undertow. It is as if the text has a Freudian slip within it, and the important thing about Freudian slips is that they do not work randomly. There is something else haunting the image of Marina's innocent prowess, and her eventual superiority in her sexual identity and her marriage prospects is evident even in her sewing. Again, there is a faint implication that something is faintly implied: in carrying off its presentation of an entirely laudable and worthy character the text makes some edgy gestures.

In *Cymbeline* the problem is a different one, and follows from two children of opposite sexes growing up together:

> The King, he takes the babe
> To his protection, calls him Posthumus Leonatus,
> Breeds him, and makes him of his bedchamber;
> Puts to him all the learnings that his time
> Could make him the receiver of, which he took
> As we do air, fast as 'twas ministered,
> And in 's spring became a harvest; lived in court—
> Which rare it is to do—most praised, most loved;
> A sample to the youngest, to th' more mature
> A glass that feated them, and to the graver
> A child that guided dotards. To his mistress,
> For whom he now is banished, her own price
> Proclaims how she esteemed him and his virtue.
> By her election may be truly read
> What kind of man he is.

(1.1.40–54)

The King adopted Posthumus and he flourished into the kind of man fit to marry the King's daughter. This reflection on childhood comes from the outside, and so the kinds of intensity observed elsewhere are absent unless they are inferred. And this is a notably decorous account. Possibly those who knew a bit about court life could have imagined that an adopted boy in the King's retinue might have had limited access to the female circle around the princess. On the other hand, the complete lack of reference to the irony of the marriage or the opportunities offered by proximity is testimony to the observer's loyalty and tact—and also, it must be admitted, to the fact that such young people in Shakespeare's romances are genuinely blameless. A comparison with *The Tempest* adds a layer of potential: in that play we hear of how, in his own account, not really denied by anyone, Prospero took Caliban into his home and hoped to raise him to better things. The project was a failure, and involves a debased replay of what in *Cymbeline* is an innocent love developing within the home. However, even in *Cymbeline* the King's anger at the overlap between family ties and sexuality may seem specifically misapplied, but generally tenable.

The Two Noble Kinsmen has at its heart a number of intimate friendships—one aspect in which it follows very naturally from Shakespeare's late work, although it is a collaboration. In his other play featuring Theseus of Athens, he made nothing of the hero's mythical friendship with Pirithous: the latter does not even appear in *A Midsummer Night's Dream*. In *The Two Noble Kinsmen* he does appear, but it is other friendships that dominate. One may be seen to have inhibiting consequences, a close analogy for Leontes and Polixenes—that of Emilia and Flavina. Emilia agrees that the friendship of Theseus and Pirithous 'has more ground, is more maturely seasoned', but she and her friend were (and this is telling) 'things innocent':

> The flower that I would pluck
> And put between my breasts—O then but beginning
> To swell about the blossom—she would long
> Till she had such another, and commit it
> To the like innocent cradle, where, phoenix-like,
> They died in perfume. On my head no toy
> But was her pattern. Her affections—pretty,
> Though happily her careless wear—I followed
> For my most serious decking. Had mine ear
> Stol'n some new air, or at adventure hummed one,
> From musical coinage, why, it was a note

Whereon her spirits would sojourn—rather dwell on—
And sing it in her slumbers.

(1.3.66–78)

She goes on to say that 'the true love 'tween maid and maid may
be | More than in sex dividual'—this kind of love is better than
that between man and woman. Emilia asserts that she has no plans to
marry. Her description of idyllic days with Flavina recalls repetitive and
imitative patterns, a closed cycle of likeness which, not surprisingly,
can be seen as an inhibiting force in her adulthood. The complexity of
her verse in the quotation above, the parentheses and enjambments, as
well as the vividness of the description, testify to how alive the past is
for her, in comparison with her rather still demeanour in the present
of the play. She speaks with the same reverent nostalgia as Polixenes
when he recalls his innocent childhood—and the two episodes tell
us something beyond characters, about the texture of the romance
idyll, and how precarious its perfect solutions are under pressure from
reality and mortality.

The friendship of Palamon and Arcite is fundamental to the
play and it is at the heart of its main source, Chaucer's *Knight's
Tale*. Ann Thompson's study of Shakespeare and Chaucer finds that
Shakespeare's parts of the play rethink Chaucer in a deeper way
than Fletcher's.[11] Nevertheless the whole play participates in the
development of the friendship theme. The two are so close as to
exclude others, to a dysfunctional extent. One aspect of this is that
they are seen to act as something other than friends:

> It seems to me they have no more sense of their captivity than I of
> ruling Athens. They eat well, look merrily, discourse of many things,
> but nothing of their own restraint and disasters. Yet sometime a divided
> sigh—martyred as 'twere i'th' deliverance—will break from one of them,
> when the other presently gives it so sweet a rebuke that I could wish
> myself a sigh to be so chid, or at least a sigher to be comforted.

(2.1.37–45)

The speaker here is the Jailer's Daughter, who has a hopeless love
for Palamon which may be reflected in her vision of happy captivity
and behaviour. However, it does not contrast with what we see.
The description of sighing and sweet rebuking and wanting nothing
more than one another's company makes them sound like lovers.

There is nothing sexual between them—and their intensity is not unimaginable—but there is some resemblance to classic lovers such as Romeo and Juliet, and their tragedy may also strike a similar note. A friendship stretched to breaking point is the heart of the play's most moving moments. Here one makes sure the other is well-armed for battle, a scene they must have shared before—but this time the battle is between them:

> Will't please you arm, sir?
> Or, if you feel yourself not fitting yet,
> And furnished with your old strength, I'll stay, cousin,
> And every day discourse you into health,
> As I am spared. Your person I am friends with,
> And I could wish I had not said I loved her,
> Though I had died; but loving such a lady,
> And justifying my love, I must not fly from't.
>
> (3.6.35–42)

There is a tragic quality in the situation created by a clash between the bond of friendship and a chivalric code that means they must fight over Emilia. Despite the death of Arcite the play finds a way around this crisis in an untragic, tragicomic way. Intense youthful friendship is a marginal force impinging on the main action in *The Winter's Tale*, but here, in collaboration with Fletcher, Shakespeare has brought it into central focus. Its power is not an aberration in the same way, as the play has a role for all the energy generated by it.

These plays have psychological plots on their surfaces. In all cases one could argue that a certain neurosis or dysfunction must be resolved through a greater dedication to a rightful role. Leontes, then, learns to accept his roles as husband and father in an adult world, and is rewarded with the return of what he lost. What I have been trying to tease out is the way that these psychological plots have their own psychological plots. Character provides a more concrete and straightforward focus for psychoanalytic criticism, but if the focus turns to the form of the literary text, or to its readers and audiences, we can see the insidious, strange, and productive ways in which the normal passages of thought are accompanied by something else. Different desires and different anxieties lurk at the edge of these plays. This is felt in the very fabric of their language, which critics have seen as both more complex than that of earlier plays and notably striking in its power to name things and convey emotion.[12] The spiritual successes of central characters are all the more acceptable because we know that such things are always hard won and do not necessarily silence every nagging voice. Leontes famously explains that the thing which is really wrong with him is that he is not unaware. He uses an arresting image of a man drinking from a cup with a spider inside:

> There may be in the cup
> A spider steeped, and one may drink, depart,
> And yet partake no venom, for his knowledge
> Is not infected; but if one present
> Th' abhorred ingredient to his eye, make known
> How he hath drunk, he cracks his gorge, his sides,
> With violent hefts. I have drunk, and seen the spider.
>
> (2.1.41–7)

These lines could offer a paradigm of reading plays such as these. They may counsel against reading in straight lines, against taking anything at face value. In doing so they hint that the things discovered by such a technique could be dark and fearful. Once the spider has been seen, reality is redefined; once one reads in the same way, the plays can never look the same again. However, it matters that it is Leontes who proposes the analogy. Readers of Shakespeare's late work should not drift through, ignorant of what lurks within, but we should remember that Leontes' paranoid, obsessive viewpoint is not the one to emulate. The spectrum of reality taken in by Shakespeare's late work is wider than romance can accommodate simply. The complexity that results enriches the plays and challenges readers to choose how much they want to see.

Conservative Endings

Shakespeare's late plays feature drastic action and turbulent personal journeys. To some extent it is paradoxical that the world that emerges from the action is very similar to, or follows naturally from, the one that preceded it. This is particularly true of the plays' social structures: the twists and turns of fortune are not reflected in new configurations of power or a greater mobility between groups. Rather, once-truncated royal bloodlines are restored and consolidated by advantageous marriages, and power is passed on. In addition, the good characters in whom moral hopes reside turn out to be related to the ruling families of the plays. There is little of the discovered virtue that one can see in comedy, or of the discovered sin one finds in tragedy: eventually the powerful find validation, albeit in traumatic ways. As Northrop Frye said of romance in general, there may be a 'pervasive social snobbery'.[1] The possible conservatism of the romances stands in contrast with the plays that precede them. *Timon of Athens* and *Coriolanus* are notably negative about society and its institutions. This tendency takes a variety of forms. Neither of these plays proposes much faith in human nature, and neither places greater hope in the well-born, who tend to be isolated or corrupt—by no means the central point in an organic, cooperative society. We also see tension between different classes, political activism, and people straining against the inherited order.[2] In Shakespeare's late work, whether because of genre or conceptual shift, things are different.

It is possible that the notion of social mobility, or its absence, has no place in an audience's or reader's experience of these works, or indeed of any romance. The genre itself may prize restoration and continuity rather than change or progress, and it may be an imposition to begin worrying about the conservatism of the political structure of the plays. There is a distinctive, repeated, very clear emphasis in late Shakespeare on the inherent virtue of characters who turn out to be nobly born. What first appears as a wonder—the nobility of Perdita, Guiderius, and Arviragus in their pastoral disguises—merely makes sense in the end. This is part of the excitement of the plays' conclusions, a source of pleasure as things come together in a providential plan. It may also be a little downbeat, even debilitating: after so much energy, things return to their fixed state. This chapter will set out these moments of perhaps excessive trust in the inherent goodness of the noble characters, in order to consider their significance as part of the exploratory dynamics of late Shakespeare. It will also outline ways in which more energetic, more inclusive forces impinge on the settled social structure of the romance ending. Both sides of the argument are sharpened by the contemporary political context of the later works. They provide parallels and alternatives to King James I's promotion of his own family as a vital new dynasty. These plays were performed at court as well as on the public stage, so such ideas have multiple contexts and implications.

The Winter's Tale involves the most explicit exploration of these themes. The sheep-shearing festival scene in Bohemia involves a disguised prince (who knows his identity, and others know it too), a disguised princess (unwitting and unrecognized, except by the audience), and also a lengthy hypothetical discussion about horticulture that rehearses ideas about the desirability of mixing royal blood with common. The prince and princess, Florizel and Perdita, have fallen in love. The scene starts with them discussing their unfamiliar clothing. She is dressed as queen of the festival, while he is in shepherd's garb:

> FLORIZEL   These your unusual weeds to each part of you
>   Does give a life; no shepherdess, but Flora
>   Peering in April's front. This your sheep-shearing
>   Is as a meeting of the petty gods,
>   And you the queen on't.
> PERDITA   Sir, my gracious lord,
>   To chide at your extremes it not becomes me—
>   O, pardon that I name them! Your high self,
>   The gracious mark o'th' land, you have obscured
>   With a swain's wearing, and me, poor lowly maid,

Most goddess-like pranked up. But that our feasts
In every mess have folly, and the feeders
Digest it with a custom, I should blush
To see you so attired; swoon, I think,
To show myself a glass.

(4.4.1–14)

Florizel has no similar worry, and advises her to 'apprehend nothing but jollity' (15). From his elevated social position the transformation is not troubling, but for Perdita it is less comfortable, even though her true identity is actually reflected better in her new clothing. This is not an innocent irony: in the implied logic of these moments in Shakespeare's romances some are born great, but nobody becomes great or has greatness thrust upon them. Later in the scene Autolycus, the wandering minstrel-thief who has a courtly past, also considers clothing in relation to nobility:

> Whether it like me or no, I am a courtier. Seest thou not the air of the court in these enfoldings? Hath not my gait in it the measure of the court? Receives not thy nose court-odour from me? Reflect I not on thy baseness court-contempt? Thinkest thou, for that I insinuate to toze from thee thy business, I am therefore no courtier? I am courtier cap-à-pie, and one that will either push on or pluck back thy business there. Whereupon I command thee to open thy affair.

(4.4.730–8)

At this point Autolycus is trying to bamboozle the Shepherd and the Clown (Perdita's adoptive father and brother) into telling him the latest developments. He hopes to gain advantage from the knowledge, and his courtly disguise allows him to promise he can help the rustic pair in their alarming visit to the court. The tables are turned on him later in the play, when the revelation of Perdita's true parenthood leads to an honorary ennoblement for her Bohemian family. The Clown tells Autolycus that he has been 'a gentleman born' for some 'four hours' (5.2.136). Again clothing is decisive: his new rich outfit affects his status to the extent of, comically, altering his birth to a noble one. This amusing by-play has a rather sharp relationship with the notions of birth and nobility evoked by Perdita and Florizel. The audience is under no illusion that clothes can really make nobles of the Clown and Autolycus—their reflections on the matter even get in the way of the possibility that the Shepherd's kindness and steadfastness might indeed earn him moral nobility. Instead, they are a travesty of the true nobility that cannot be hidden in those of genuinely elevated descent.

The horticultural argument of 4.4 sees Polixenes and Perdita take sides in a debate about the value of tampering with nature. While this does indeed tackle weighty philosophical issues—the relationship of art and nature—it is also a curiously empty argument. Perdita argues against herself (as a shepherdess) by saying that one should not corrupt strains of plants by grafting. This is taken by Polixenes to be a denial of socially mixed marriage. This could be an energetic topic, but it does not become so: there is a rather flat irony that her interests are in fact served by the argument of conservative purity. The hollow note that sounds faintly here is stronger when Perdita describes what looks like an egalitarian rejoinder to the King's threats of punishment:

> I was not much afeard, for once or twice
> I was about to speak, and tell him plainly
> The selfsame sun that shines upon his court
> Hides not his visage from our cottage, but
> Looks on alike.
>
> (4.4.442–6)

Perhaps this statement's pertinence and its spirited denial of old hierarchy survive its context, but this is a fragile hope. The unwitting princess validates her own eventual emergence; the sun, after all, shines more brightly on her than on her adoptive family. Her inherent virtue outshines her supposed equals, and nature trounces nurture, whatever the subtleties attending her argument with the King.

The same pattern is evident elsewhere in late Shakespeare. In *The Two Noble Kinsmen*, for example, the Jailer's Daughter's love for Palamon is inconceivable. She is a very complex character, marooned in her darkly comic subplot but herself a rather tragic figure who barely sees her love. However, the question of her desire for a Theban prince is simple: it is not viable. *Cymbeline* is an interesting case because of Innogen's illicit marriage to Posthumus. He is not of royal blood, but he is of comfortably noble heritage. He also has two saving characteristics: one is that he is not remotely ambitious and never connects marriage to Innogen with heightened status. The other is that he does not become King, and happily gives way to the rediscovered Princes. It is Cloten who is the upstart despite being a Prince by marriage; he has responded less well to courtly nurture than his rival. A clearer and more resounding handling of the issue of noble virtue comes in the story of Guiderius and Arviragus, royal Princes kidnapped by a courtier (Belarius) who has a justified, if not clearly proportionate, grievance. He brings them up in rural simplicity and they have no idea of their ancestry, but Belarius keeps noticing their birth asserting itself:

> How hard it is to hide the sparks of nature!
> These boys know little they are sons to th' King,
> Nor Cymbeline dreams that they are alive.
> They think they are mine, and though trained up thus meanly
> I'th' cave wherein they bow, their thoughts do hit
> The roofs of palaces, and nature prompts them
> In simple and low things to prince it much
> Beyond the trick of others.

(3.3.79–86)

One brother is enraptured by stories of martial heroism and acts out his own natural prowess. The other shows a skill in language, improving on Belarius's own storytelling with his inherent eloquence and wisdom. It is not difficult for a literary audience or reader to understand this: this is a kind of pastoral, where something greater is contained in a rural scene. However it is also a little skewed. Belarius is a nobleman, a warrior, and a wise man. His absolute faith that the boys' talents are due to birth rather than himself and his virtuous wife seems odd; it could perhaps reflect modesty, or guilt at his crime. The ascetic idyll in which they have been raised might be hailed as ideal for fostering such qualities, especially in conventional contrast with the corrupt court.

The play may allow some resistance to the idea that virtue and true royal birth are deeply connected, but it offers the idea strongly none the less. Belarius, after all, returns to his theme in an aside a little later in the play:

> O noble strain!
> O worthiness of nature, breed of greatness!
> Cowards father cowards, and base things sire base.
> Nature hath meal and bran, contempt and grace.
> I'm not their father, yet who this should be
> Doth miracle itself, loved before me.

(4.2.24–9)

These last two lines concern the ailing boy for whom the two youths have conceived a wondrous affection. It is actually their lost sister Innogen, which neither they nor Belarius know. Their innate blood-bond creates a sympathy that seems to cause their supposed father envy. Belarius comes across as less secure here, as if his self-reflexive praise of his impressive pseudo-sons is being outmanoeuvred by the evident strength of the characteristics bestowed upon them by birth. He continues on his theme once more:

> O thou goddess,
> Thou divine Nature, how thyself thou blazon'st
> In these two princely boys! They are as gentle
> As zephyrs blowing below the violet,
> Not wagging his sweet head; and yet as rough,
> Their royal blood enchafed, as the rud'st wind
> That by the top doth take the mountain pine
> And make him stoop to th' vale. 'Tis wonder
> That an invisible instinct should frame them
> To royalty unlearned, honour untaught,
> Civility not seen from other, valour
> That wildly grows in them, but yields a crop
> As if it had been sowed.

> (4.2.170–82)

It is possible to construct a psychological reading of this: Belarius is dogged by the knowledge of his unnatural crime and keeps seeing supposed evidence of it. However, one may also still wonder about other reasons for this repeated emphasis on the connection between elevated birth and noble character. A useful comparison might be Ulysses' speech on 'degree' in *Troilus and Cressida* (1.3.74–137), which serves as an archetypal demonstration of the ordered cosmos and the 'great chain of being' in E. M. W. Tillyard's *The Elizabethan World-Picture*.[3] Modern critics are often sceptical about treating this ideological exposition of the need for observing hierarchy as an authentic expression of how Shakespeare or his audience saw the world. In *Troilus and Cressida*, for example, we note that Ulysses is the great political schemer and his speech serves to pin down and promote a course of action in the Greek camp: the principles espoused are energetic, contestable, pragmatic, and productive, not descriptive. How this bears on the romances is difficult to pin down: it is right to recognize the discordant notes struck within and against this idea of the nature of nobility, but it is also important to note the force of the repetition and the way it fits with the romance mode. Shakespeare reaches out for and expands upon a certainty contained within the logic of romance, but as that certainty grows it becomes more volatile and begins to defeat itself. In this case it is clear that when such a principle defeats itself life, ironically, is affirmed: and this kind of ironic affirmation is typical of late Shakespeare.

In Shakespeare's romances birth is never said to matter more than worth, but the point is moot—birth and worth are the same thing. The romances include huge ruptures in royal succession, but the only option is to recover what has been lost—the alternative monarchies that arise are tyrannical. One reason for this could be some important contemporary resonances in these plots. After Elizabeth's childless death and the fears before the event as to what would happen, King James I introduced into English life a royal family in which the nation could invest its hopes. This process was not without friction as he imported his own court from Scotland, but by the time of *Pericles* the national mythology was beginning to adapt to a family rather than a solitary, virgin queen. The young heir apparent, Prince Henry, a patron of the arts and an aspirant military hero, soon became the embodiment of Protestant hopes that England would become an aggressive player in European politics. David Bergeron has argued for specific connections between James's family and the royal families of the late plays.[4] James promoted himself as a central father figure, and Shakespeare may be testing out that ideological construction—in the end it passes the test. Bergeron sees the royal family as a text rather than as a historical fact: something with themes and dynamics, and it is these that are fertile for Shakespeare's work, rather than specific events or issues. This is a very resourceful way of characterizing the extent to which the romances are 'about' politics. They constantly interact with themes and structures in the royal story.

For Bergeron, the period between 1607 and 1613, the period of Shakespeare's late work, included the heyday and the crucial crisis of the royal family. In 1607 the established King retained hope of an Act of Union between England and Scotland; Henry had been invested as Prince of Wales; things were going well on the whole. However, tensions between the father and his family grew; the Act of Union did not happen until 1707; and the greatest disappointment was the death of Henry in 1612, leading to national mourning. The romances are written through this period. Three of the four (not *Pericles*), as well as (possibly) *The Two Noble Kinsmen* and *Henry VIII*, were performed at the wedding celebrations of Princess Elizabeth and Duke Frederick the Elector Palatine in early 1613—so they were involved in the royal family's recovery from the trauma of 1612. We cannot know the extent to which the plays were adapted for these performances, or indeed whether the versions we have show the results of that adaptation. Clearly the courtly audience might have been sensitive to tactless mention of dead brothers, while it may also have been delighted by attention to daughters and their prospects. Some believe *The Winter's Tale* as it survives, with Hermione not dead, is a revision for just such a purpose.[5] The possibility of court performance and even revision for such performances offers a reminder that the political texture of these plays might not reflect the author's search for stability. It may be a politic exploration, with some awkward questions emerging here and there, of a set of ideas that would be gratifying to the monarch and the prevailing mood.

At which point it seems natural to search for moments where the political texture gets a bit rougher. Modern readings of *The Tempest* often discover more political energy.[6] Caliban embodies the nature/nurture debate rehearsed by Polixenes and Perdita in *The Winter's Tale*. Where there it was a desultory debate based on misunderstanding, in Shakespeare's next play it is more sharply ambiguous. Prospero has tried nurture, but concludes that nature is dominant:

> Thou most lying slave,
> Whom stripes may move, not kindness! I have used thee,
> Filth as thou art, with human care, and lodged thee
> In mine own cell, till thou didst seek to violate
> The honour of my child.

> (1.2.346–50)

The charge of attempted rape is not denied. A modern reader of the play might struggle with the scene in the light of the history of colonialism. The idea, proposed by Prospero but not straightforwardly by Shakespeare, that a colonial subject might be naturally degenerate, is, for us, discredited. Acts of brutality such as Caliban's foiled rape might be explained as the product of a process of brutalization. On the other hand, there are sharp edges to the nature and nurture question in the play. Any modern scruples about condemning Caliban cannot easily escape the play's basic self-vindication in its treatment of Prospero's slave, and the quasi-facts behind it. Miranda joins her father in condemning a failed project:

> I pitied thee,
> Took pains to make thee speak, taught thee each hour
> One thing or other. When thou didst not, savage,
> Know thine own meaning, but wouldst gabble like
> A thing most brutish, I endowed thy purposes
> With words that made them known. But thy vile race,
> Though thou didst learn, had that in't which good natures
> Could not abide to be with; therefore wast thou
> Deservedly confined into this rock,
> Who hadst deserved more than a prison.
>
> (1.2.355–64)

Eighteenth- and nineteenth-century editors of this scene sometimes transferred this speech to Prospero, discomfited by harsh words in Miranda's supposedly tender mouth.[7] But it is very important that she shares in her father's opinion and his rhetoric. The telling qualification ('Though thou didst learn') is an uncomfortable admission. Caliban's twofold reaction to this teaching of language is first, to reject it and to relish only the ability to curse, and second, more subtly, to manifest linguistic inventiveness and poetic aptitude when describing the island. The interplay of nature and nurture is far more complex than Prospero or Miranda allow—than they can afford to allow, given the extent to which they benefit from the power-structure that is validated by the rejection of Caliban.

Prospero commands the island, but this new space, full of potential, prompts others to consider how they would rule it. For Caliban this is a desperate longing for what he sees as a usurped birthright. He gets his wish in the end, though the play gives no hint as to what the future holds or how he feels about it. Stefano and Trinculo, in their drunkenness, conceive their ideal island as a place of free music and wine. It is revealing that the most fully articulated vision of the island is not a self-serving or repressive one, but the idealistic fantasy of Gonzalo:

> I'th' commonwealth I would by contraries
> Execute all things. For no kind of traffic
> Would I admit, no name of magistrate;
> Letters should not be known; riches, poverty,
> And use of service, none; contract, succession,
> Bourn, bound of land, tilth, vineyard, none;
> No use of metal, corn, or wine, or oil;
> No occupation, all men idle, all;
> And women too—but innocent and pure;
> No sovereignty—

> (2.1.148–57)

And at this point the cynical Sebastian interjects 'Yet he would be king on't'. Gonzalo's more or less absurd Utopian reverie fails to operate as a counterweight to a conservative and positive presentation of the idea that noble birth correlates with noble behaviour. The well-meaning courtier is trapped in static pleasantries at best ('all men idle'). As a result the audience might gain a deeper appreciation of the practicalities of power. Renaissance political theory, as in the work of Machiavelli, or the pragmatic elements of Francis Bacon's *Essays*, challenges straightforward moral censure by being tuned into reality and necessity. One of Bacon's *Essays* does, in fact, consider the issue of how to handle a space such as Prospero's island. In 'Of Plantations', Bacon regulates the place of women in his plantation. After emphasizing the need to exploit the potential for fertile growth, he states that 'when the plantation grows to strength, then it is time, to plant with women, as well as with men', with the result that the place 'may spread into generations'.[8] Prospero's land of sterile illusion does not resemble this. The island of *The Tempest* also breaks another of Bacon's rules:

> I like a plantation in a pure soil; that is, where people are not displaced, to the end, to plant in others. For else, it is rather an extirpation, than a plantation.

> (106)

Bacon's essays are 'civil or moral'; in fact they combine civil and moral, exploring the compromise between the conclusions one would like to draw, and the ones that reality will actually allow. His plan for a plantation is no more real than Prospero's island, but its strictures are practical: to perpetrate 'extirpation' is wrong because it brings trouble.

Gonzalo's rumination is nothing at all like Bacon, and Antonio and Sebastian are right when they note how it meanders. His plan is to start again without nobility, but astute observers know this cannot be done. The late plays' espousal of a conservative idea as to the nature of nobility might partly derive from, and belong in, a knowledge that this is not how one would wish the world to be at all.

There are still some facts that remain. Prospero is the true Duke, Miranda and Ferdinand are rightly joined, Alonso must see the error of his ways, while Antonio's failure to do so explicitly may be allowed as one of the inevitable disruptions that result from human frailty. Nevertheless, the world often falls into place with Prospero's plan even more neatly than a well-made strategy deserves. Modern critics and audiences are surely right to allow their interest to veer towards alternative models of the world, if only for temporary release from the play's controlled plot. Similarly, when in *Cymbeline* Belarius returns yet again to his refrain about the unquenchable nobility of his pseudo-sons, the audience might think 'why go on about it?' There is a crucial difference here from the protestations of Orlando in Shakespeare's much earlier *As You Like It*. That play opens with the young hero lamenting his state, comparing himself to a beast, complaining that he is being kept in a manner far beneath the dignity of his birth (1.1.1–23). He is accompanied by the elderly servant Adam, whose acceptance that it is naturally and inevitably true that Orlando must live a better life than his might not be taken for granted. Nor might that of the audience. In this case, however, Orlando clearly has something to learn: the play will smooth off the peevish immaturity. In the late romances, the action only validates the confidence of characters in the worth of birth.

It has proved very fertile in recent criticism and performance to look for moments of strain in *The Tempest*. At the forefront has been the reinterpretation of Caliban, but one must also look to the strained service of Ariel, Prospero's moments of anxiety, and indeed to the recalcitrance of Antonio and Sebastian, or the base humdrum failings of Stefano and Trinculo. These all offer different forms of freedom or potential that prove salutary even if the ultimate conclusion is the only way forward.[9] Annabel Patterson, for example, discovers some role for the 'popular voice' in the play. She starts from the recognition that the late plays may indeed withdraw from the radicalism of *Timon* and

Coriolanus: 'Must we, then, draw the conclusion that after *Coriolanus*, in which Shakespeare challenged the very structure of his society, he retreated to the philosophical aristocracy of which, according to Coleridge, he had always been a member?'[10] Patterson sees Coleridge as the originator of the idea that Shakespeare had little respect for popular politics. However, even in the late plays she sees room for manoeuvre, and answers her own question 'Not necessarily'. A key moment for Patterson is Stefano's song that means so much to Caliban when it asserts that 'thought is free' (3.2.125)—there are places in the play where social energy can find a voice. This works despite the fact that Prospero explicitly inhibits potential and novelty at a critical moment:

> MIRANDA   O wonder!
>   How many goodly creatures are there here!
>   How beauteous mankind is! O brave new world
>   That has such people in't!
> PROSPERO   'Tis new to thee.
>
>   (5.1.184–7)

It is a heavy irony that Miranda's famous and much-quoted exclamation is undercut within the play. She encounters the world in a hopeful way; her belief in the 'beauteous' nature of mankind runs against her treatment of Caliban and opens the possibility that anybody might prove worthy. However, her statement 'How many goodly creatures are there here!' shares the form of a question, and we as audience or readers know that the number is smaller than the total present. Her father also knows the answer, and this lies behind his response: ' 'Tis new to thee.' The framework of experience and hierarchy is quickly reasserted, and Miranda does not say a word for the remainder of the play. Any freedom one could give in interpretation to the idea that *The Tempest* might enable greater hope for the ignobly born is stifled in the end, within the play's action at least, by the silencing of Caliban and Miranda—unlikely allies. However, Prospero's corrective could be seen as gentle and nurturing: rather than grimly denying his daughter's hope, he may be giving one of his last lessons in the transition from innocence to experience.

   Another place to look for energy in these plays is in their language. Simon Palfrey's study of *Pericles*, *Cymbeline*, *The Winter's Tale*, and *The Tempest* argues against the decorousness of earlier views of these works.[11] He argues that in previous criticism there has been too much trust, both of the language of the plays and of their political make-up. So Palfrey sees a rather different atmosphere from the political inertia described above, and sees an edgier interaction between the plays and the conservatism of their genre: 'These works are not satisfied by the cursory patriarchalism of the generic skeleton, any more than their heroines are the inert vessels of a wistful pastoral ideal' (229). The young women of the plays are not easily idealized: they have too much to say for themselves, and there is too much energy latent in what they say. In his argument Caliban offers the most potential for social novelty and subversion, and overall the plays are radical and unpredictable: 'One ends with an image of incipience, an almost Yeatsian sense of the beast stirring into life, uncertain whether into grace or vice, brutal or dignifying community' (265). Such an approach points at ways in which the plays offer moments of doubt that make the kind of conservatism I have been noting seem brittle. Political energy is there to be discovered, but it takes a very energetic critic to uncover it. The tendency to limit social mobility is still noteworthy. At times readers might feel constrained by the repeating formula equating birth and worth, but this on its own validates radical and oppositional reading aimed at finding alternative ideologies.

It is not only in the four romances that one can find the conservative assumptions, and the energetic fringes, of political texture that are at issue in this chapter. The problem of succession is approached from a rather different angle in *Henry VIII* but many of the same assumptions are in evidence. The similarities between the trial of Queen Katherine and the trial of Hermione are considerable. There is the same strained dignity in their speeches in the face of hostile and unstoppable accusations. In *The Winter's Tale* Hermione refers to the fact that she is of royal descent and deserves better treatment (3.2.39). Katherine says something similar:

> The King your father was reputed for
> A prince most prudent, of an excellent
> And unmatched wit and judgement. Ferdinand
> My father, King of Spain, was reckoned one
> The wisest prince that there had reigned by many
> A year before.

$$(2.4.43-8)$$

Henry is guided not to fall short of his father's wisdom. He is also presented with the attractive logic of family continuity and inherent noble worth. Of course, Katherine's argument is self-serving, but in comparison with the pragmatism of her accusers she seems relatively principled. So her appeal to a fellow royal on the basis of the nature of nobility appears sincere. It is not surprising that the King, later in the scene, echoes her with a belief that royal actions accompany royal lineage:

> Thou art alone—
> If thy rare qualities, sweet gentleness,
> Thy meekness saint-like, wife-like government,
> Obeying in commanding, and thy parts
> Sovereign and pious else could speak thee out—
> The queen of earthly queens. She's noble born,
> And like her true nobility she has
> Carried herself towards me.
>
> (2.4.133–9)

He lists her virtues sincerely, but the impression is that the really affecting thing is that Katherine has impressed her nobility upon him. This strikes a chord, and creates an affinity that briefly separates the King from his lower-born political advisers. The two kinds of nobility, from birth and from worth, briefly come into conjunction. As in *The Winter's Tale* members of other social groups offer little reason to break this social order. *Henry VIII* awards the crowd, the corporate manifestation of the popular voice, little dignity when it comes to praise the King and celebrate the birth of the Princess in 5.3. A weightier variation on the theme comes in the tragic rise and fall of Wolsey. His enemies disparage his humble birth and after his undoing he too connects his failure with his overreaching:

> I have ventured,
> Like little wanton boys that swim on bladders,
> This many summers in a sea of glory,
> But far beyond my depth; my high-blown pride
> At length broke under me, and now has left me
> Weary, and old with service, to the mercy
> Of a rude stream that must for ever hide me.
>
> (3.2.359–65)

Within the logic of the social fabric of this play, there is a profound, though awkward, truth behind his image of boys carried beyond their depths by flotation devices. When he charges Cromwell to 'fling away ambition' (3.2.441) his advice has many nuances. It is moral—pride comes before a fall—and it is practical. It also accepts the play's implicit equation of high birth and high worth.

Henry VIII offers a tense form of validation for James I. It approves the status quo and it approves its restoration through tangential or miraculous means. In the other romances it is possible to imagine James in the light of both relief at the solution of a rupture in the English succession, and optimism about a new royal family. *Henry VIII* reprises both themes, and in fact explicitly invokes the succession of James as part of the glorious future attending the infant Princess Elizabeth, who is born in Act 5. However, *Henry VIII* shows its origins as a play written after the heyday of optimism in the new Stuarts. In particular, it may well have been written and was certainly performed after the death of Prince Henry, which offered a grim backdrop to hopes for the future. Whether because of the Prince's death, or because times had changed, or because a history play necessitates a different perspective from a romance, *Henry VIII* does offer a different qualification to the flaccid approval of aristocracy. The notes of anxiety that haunt the romances—yet do not quite drown out the stress on noble birth—acquire a more concrete form because subsequent history is already known. Unlike *The Winter's Tale*, there is no room for trust in subsequent centuries of joyous succession and prosperity. Cranmer's prophecy spoken over the newborn Elizabeth goes on to say that she will die without an heir, but it does not shy away at this point, and describes the succession of James I:

> He shall flourish,
> And like a mountain cedar reach his branches
> To all the plains about him. Our children's children
> Shall see this, and bless heaven.

> (5.4.52–5)

This speech has already been discussed in Chapter 1 because of its unusual version of historical truth in general. It also presses on specific contemporary issues. The image of the cedar is recognizable from the prophecy in *Cymbeline*. This majestic tree with its spreading branches seems to offer an eloquent image of dynastic fertility. Here, though, there has been a distinct and problematic glossing-over of some memorable times preceding the succession of James. Shakespeare's audience would surely have noted the irony in his unproblematic account of a process that spread over years and made many fear little less than an apocalypse. On the other hand, as I have said, Shakespeare's late work coincided with what may have seemed like a restoration of stability, and the miracle solution represented by King James may have been appropriately represented as an invisible suture in the bloodline. However, *Henry VIII*, which holds its various episodes in tension, introduces an awkward figure to the equation in the person of Mary, daughter of Henry, and his first wife, Katherine. The Queen's expression of hope for her daughter soon before her death is not fulfilled: 'She is young, and of a noble modest nature. | I hope she will deserve well' (4.2.136–7). The Queen's wish has temporary fruition outside the play, in the memory of its audience, when Mary takes the throne in 1553. However, she has no place in the providential, Protestant narrative prophesied by Cranmer. In this case history does not validate a 'noble nature', and even within the play the emphasis shifts clearly towards Elizabeth, though not towards the fate of her mother, Anne Boleyn. *Henry VIII* ostensibly bases its view of monarchy in stability and inherent nobility, but then wears its historical revisionism on its sleeve. So the potential complacency evident in some moments of the romances is avoided.

The political outlook of late Shakespeare is timely in one of its major aspects. The focus on royal families and the mystical rights and qualities transferred from generation to generation fits in with a brief moment of optimism about royalty in early Jacobean England. In comparison with the other kinds of belief explored in this part of the book the apparent faith in royalty is less profound and less central to the emotional dynamics of the plays. Nevertheless it does provide some substantial underpinning at critical moments in the late plays. The social component of the outlook of Shakespeare's late work often appears conservative, and when the theme is explored in any detail, it soon appears inert and restrictive. Rediscovery, reunion, and the eventual restoration of fit unions between well-born people—these are all aspects of the romance mode that Shakespeare embraces. However, he also resists them, incorporating within these plays moments of energy as well as an evident static quality in the principle of birth-equals-worth. As with the other kinds of belief advanced in his late work, Shakespeare invests energy in the action and the reaction, basing the plays in substance and hope, but basing the audience's interpretation in liberated irony.

Shakespeare, Middleton, and Fletcher

As was set out in the Introduction, Shakespeare's late work is partly collaborative. It also marks the end of a period in which Shakespeare dominated his company, the King's Men, and the beginning of other ascendancies. In his book *The School of Shakespeare* David Frost chooses Thomas Middleton as Shakespeare's true heir, the writer who best represents the continuing legacy of Shakespeare.[1] He does so because in Middleton's later tragedies, Frost argues, the moral order of Shakespearian tragedy is preserved—that is, action, character, and environment are all infected with sin and disaster. There is much to dispute in this. Middleton's tragedies may indeed show the contagion and pervasion of evil, but they tend to treat evil as something endemic in a corrupt world, always liable to metamorphose and return again. In Shakespeare's tragedies, more often, one might argue, evil arises without full explanation and the plays' worlds (Venice and Cyprus in *Othello*, Britain in *Lear*, Denmark in *Hamlet*, Scotland in *Macbeth*) are left denuded of all energy by the end. In Frost's account Beaumont and Fletcher are treated rather scornfully, and are not seen to have meditated seriously on Shakespeare.[2] As will be seen, I think Fletcher's works in particular, but the Beaumont–Fletcher canon more generally, are full of insight into Shakespeare, even if the tragic dimension is not always at the forefront. Nevertheless, Middleton is a presence in and around, as well as after, late Shakespeare. Or rather, unlike Fletcher who participates in a harmonious collaboration with Shakespeare, Middleton haunts the fringes of the late Shakespearian canon.

There have been great problems in identifying Middleton's works because of the tendency towards anonymous or misattributed publication of many plays. Nevertheless, thanks to the stylometric analyses of scholars such as David Lake and MacDonald Jackson, a canon of single-authored and collaborative plays has more or less coalesced from close analysis of linguistic features.[3] The most important conclusion in relation to late Shakespeare is that Middleton is the sole author of the play known as *The Second Maiden's Tragedy*. As will be seen, Middleton's revivals of Shakespeare are never simple. Shakespeare's body of work, the 'corpus', proves vulnerable to Middleton's necromantic and even necrophilic imitations and interventions—and these metaphors are indeed present literally in his Shakespearian works. *The Second Maiden's Tragedy* is a very sharp reflection on *The Winter's Tale*, replaying the statue scene and the presence of an artist in a way that is both homage and travesty. Middleton also has a hand in two plays on the fringes of the late Shakespearian canon, *Timon of Athens* and *Macbeth*. However, his first interaction with Shakespeare comes very early in his career, in *The Ghost of Lucrece* (1600), a poem that may date from his student days. Even in this obscure early work, a passionate complaint from Lucrece's ghost, there is a telling necromantic quality in the relationship with Shakespeare. Middleton restores the voice of a dead Shakespearian character in the form of a ghost.

Other unusual positions for an author in relation to another corpus can be seen in the two Shakespeare plays—*Macbeth* and *Timon of Athens*—that have Middleton in them. The Hecate scenes in *Macbeth* contain songs also found in Middleton's play *The Witch*. This play is of uncertain date, but could come from as late as 1615, and clearly post-dates *Macbeth*. The adaptation, then, could even date from after Shakespeare's death. Whatever the date, it is a natural hypothesis that these sections (3.5 and parts of 4.1), which are extraneous to the main structure of the play, are Middleton's. Their greatest contribution to the play is the opportunity for music and dancing. Modern taste is a little resistant to generic mixing, but it does not seem unsympathetic to note the incongruity of these particular dances and songs. These scenes include songs taken from their natural home in Middleton's *The Witch* but also linking dialogue that is sometimes perfunctory. It is rather harsh to blame Middleton for these lines, since they could have been inserted by any jobbing writer employed to graft the songs into the play for a special performance. One plausible scenario is that at some point in 1615 or 1616 *Macbeth* was reworked to be played at court in front of the King.[4] A greater emphasis on witchcraft would gratify the author of *Daemonologie*.[5] Act 3 Scene 5 in particular has a supplementary character, and it even seems to extract irony from that:

HECATE   Saucy and over-bold, how did you dare
          To trade and traffic with Macbeth
          In riddles and affairs of death,
          And I, the mistress of your charms,
          The close contriver of all harms,
          Was never called to bear my part
          Or show the glory of our art?

(3.5.3–9)

This is a question rather easily answered, if these scenes are not by Shakespeare. There is heavy irony here as a suspicious character actually advertises her own irrelevance, or protests at her omission by the play first time round. One might credit the adapter of the play with this irony, though it could be a perfunctory attempt to make sense of Hecate's intervention. Again the dancing and singing are the point. Middleton's role in *Macbeth* is uncertain—it is not possible to ascertain whether the works of two authors were grafted with the consent and interest of one or neither. However, it does compare with his interaction with Shakespeare's œuvre elsewhere. In *Macbeth* as we receive it Middleton is a parasite in the corpus, awkwardly placed and curiously assertive.

His role in writing *Timon of Athens* can be more securely mapped out.[6] John Jowett's edition of the play has both developed the idea that it is a genuine collaboration, and explored differences in the contributions of the two authors. He finds that Middleton is more satirical than Shakespeare in his sections. His Timon is a 'reckless prodigal' who squanders money, and whose downfall has a comic element.[7] This may lead towards the remarkable thing about the tone of *Timon*—overall and especially of Shakespeare's parts. It has the structure of satire without the pleasure and triumph of satire. The turn towards community that satire can take, even in its bitterest forms—reader and writer at some stage share a view of the target—does not come into being. This case of dual authorship does not show the same characteristics as the other key collaboration of the latter part of Shakespeare's career—that with Fletcher. This was not, it seems from internal evidence, typical of the most harmonious models of multiple authorship in the period. The play that emerged bears the marks of a fragmented composition and is in the unenviable position of being a play that may never have been acted, and might not have been printed in the Folio, had it not been for problems with securing copy for *Troilus and Cressida*.[8]

It is in *The Second Maiden's Tragedy* that Middleton comes closest to late Shakespeare. This play dates from *c*.1611 and is therefore in close proximity to Shakespearian romance. One scene seems to revisit the famous moment of revival from *The Winter's Tale*, but Middleton does not focus on the marvellous transformation of Hermione. Rather he revisits the physical curiosity-value of the scrutinized statue. The conclusion to the main plot sees Govianus pretending to be an artist and painting poison on the lips of his dead lover, in order to kill the Tyrant, who has necrophilic intentions. This episode recalls, in a strange and parodic way, the invented story of the statue of Hermione in *The Winter's Tale*. Whereas in Shakespeare the irony is derived from Paulina's imaginative construction of how a sculpture became so lifelike, in Middleton it has a rather different quality. For the Tyrant slavers over the thought that the Lady's death can be masked by skilful painting, and encourages Govianus to perform the job. His willingness to do so fits with his plot to deceive and poison the prince, but of course it also creates additional disgust in the audience and surely the impression of greater trauma and horror in the loving husband who has to work on his dead wife's face:

> TYRANT Let but thy art hide death upon her face,
>   That now looks fearfully on us, and but strive
>   To give our eye delight in that pale part
>   Which draws so many pities from these springs,
>   And thy reward for it shall outlast thy end,
>   And reach to thy friend's fortunes, and his friend.[9]

The paradoxical combination of a wish to 'hide death' with a plan to gain delight from 'a pale part' is a manifestation of perverted taste overlaid on the essential paradox of the statue in *The Winter's Tale*. There too the statue achieves the aim of creating liveliness out of death, and there too the human body (and the actress's body) plays a dual role. The first description of the statue comes at an additional remove from the scene in question, with Paulina's story retold by the Third Gentleman:

The Princess, hearing of her mother's statue, which is in the keeping of Paulina, a piece many years in doing, and now newly performed by that rare Italian master Giulio Romano, who, had he himself eternity and could put breath into his work, would beguile nature of her custom, so perfectly he is her ape. He so near to Hermione hath done Hermione that they say one would speak to her and stand in hope of answer.

(5.2.93–101)

This scene in *The Winter's Tale* comes before the actual unveiling of Hermione—in both plays the strain on performance is prefigured by careful preparation. The nature of Middleton's apparent response to Shakespeare is complex: he makes the motif more literal and twists it away from the unusual decorum of the Shakespearian scene.

The closeness of the interaction between *The Second Maiden's Tragedy* and *The Winter's Tale* takes a further turn when the Tyrant expresses a wish for his simulacrum to come to life. In Shakespeare the sequence starts with a gentler irony as Leontes is so moved by the appearance of the statue that he wishes to kiss it. For Paulina this causes comic panic at the thought that her plot will be revealed too early (it is worth noting that the play never investigates the fact that her subterfuge is known by the end):

LEONTES   Still methinks
    There is an air comes from her. What fine chisel
    Could ever yet cut breath? Let no man mock me,
    For I will kiss her.
PAULINA   Good my lord, forbear.
    The ruddiness upon her lip is wet.
    You'll mar it if you kiss it, stain your own
    With oily painting.

(5.3.77–83)

There are sharp edges in this scene: Leontes' desire might excite mockery but it also hints at difficult emotional undercurrents. The desire for his dead wife is partly the result of his repentance and his passionate rediscovery of what he lost. However, it is also a kind of travesty in its enthusiasm for the physical object. Middleton takes these hints and transforms them into the skittish wishes of the Tyrant, who (not surprisingly) is not satisfied with the chance to look at and kiss a dead body:

TYRANT   Could I now send for one to renew heat
   Within her bosom, that were a fine workman!
   I should but too much love him. But alas,
   'Tis as unpossible for living fire
   To take hold there,
   As for dead ashes to burn back again
   Into those hard, tough bodies whence they fell.

(5.2.96–102)

There is a rich contrast between the homiletic grimness of his discussion of the irrevocability of death, and his idea of just how grateful he would be to the 'workman' who could bring a body back to life. This is a complex psychological portrait, vividly bringing out the elements that make the Tyrant dangerous and ultimately vulnerable. Govianus has poisoned the lips of the corpse and his enemy's passion brings him death.

It is also part of a subtle interaction with Shakespeare, for the Tyrant's perversity is a refraction of Leontes' sincere bemusement, and the whole scene is a vicious travesty of what Shakespeare's play makes part of a redemptive spiritual plot. Despite his facing up to the certainty of death the Tyrant is swept up in his enthusiasm for the artist's skill in touching up the statue:

TYRANT   O, she lives again!
   She'll presently speak to me. Keep her up;
   I'll have her swoon no more; there's treachery in't.
   Does she not feel warm to thee?
GOVIANUS   Very little, sir.
TYRANT   The heat wants cherishing, then. Our arms and lips
   Shall labour life into her. Wake, sweet mistress!

(5.2.114–19)

Again there is a double edge in Govianus's perspective. His deadpan response enables a comical effect given that he is the master of the irony here. However, he is restating the fact of his wife's death and spectating on his enemy's fetishization of her corpse, so there is friction between the comical effect and the agony of his position. Both scenes recall Ovid's story of Pygmalion in *Metamorphoses* 10 — and this interaction is part of Middleton's parody, part of what he is parodying. Leontes, like Pygmalion and the Tyrant, finds warmth where he does not expect to find it:

O, she's warm!
If this be magic, let it be an art
Lawful as eating.

(5.3.109–11)

For Leontes this is a discovery, but for Pygmalion and (in a way) the Tyrant it is the result of work—they 'labour life into her'. Middleton takes what is a delicate subtext of the scene in *The Winter's Tale* and brings it to the surface. Indeed, he takes the perverted elements of the Ovidian story and makes them yet more literal. So Middleton is travestying Shakespeare and his sources, resisting the romance version of the theme and transforming it into brutal tragedy. And yet he still strikes a romance note at a climactic moment, when Govianus meets the Lady's ghost—her proper form after death and a restoration of sorts after the business with the corpse:

Enter the Ghost of the Lady
GOVIANUS   Welcome to mine eyes
As is the dayspring from the morning's womb
Unto that wretch whose nights are tedious,
As liberty to captives, health to labourers,
And life still to old people, never weary on't!

(5.2.154–8)

This echoes a number of late Shakespearian themes, both in its spring imagery and its sense of restoration: in *The Winter's Tale*, for example, Leontes says 'welcome hither, as is the spring to the earth' when he greets Florizel and Perdita (5.1.150–1). Middleton, then, picks up numerous things from Shakespeare and replays them in a very different context in *The Second Maiden's Tragedy*. The closeness between them in time suggests that Middleton is responding within an immediate theatrical milieu—*The Winter's Tale* was not yet printed, after all—making a challenge and a kind of tribute to emerging styles on the stage. Things highly characteristic of late Shakespeare are actually in evidence in other contemporary works to the extent that it is not always possible to identify Shakespeare as the inaugurator of key elements of his own style, and indeed to the extent that it is not feasible to assert a clear author-based priority in who did what first. *The Second Maiden's Tragedy* is not just aimed at *The Winter's Tale*; it is a different response to the same things Shakespeare's play is tackling.

Like Middleton, Fletcher revives Shakespeare, incorporates Shakespeare within his own body of work, and is incorporated into Shakespeare's. But instead of the sharp and antagonistic edges to Middleton's relationship with his colleague and predecessor's writings, there is a much more benign exchange. Fletcher finds an easier place within Shakespeare's corpus as a harmonious and constructive collaborator; even the notes of contention detectable within their collaborations are good-natured and part of an open exchange. His revivals of Shakespeare's works are more genial and cooperative, and never approach Middleton's necromantic travesty in *The Second Maiden's Tragedy*.

When writing about Fletcher, one is often in fact writing about 'Beaumont and Fletcher', since the two authors collaborated frequently, their collected works were and still are printed together, and some plays are only tentatively attributed one way or another, or to both. It is useful to consider in passing plays that are part of the Beaumont–Fletcher canon, but which are thought primarily to be by Beaumont. This is the case with *The Knight of the Burning Pestle*. Here a Shakespearian character walks the stage again in a travestied and ghostly form, not exactly like Lucrece or Hermione's statue, but with the same rich interplay between the thematic interests of the play and the imitation involved in its creative process. In *The Knight of the Burning Pestle* we see the ghost of Banquo's ghost. The whole play is peppered with theatrical references, and the grocer who is at the centre of it is a great theatregoer, with seven years' experience. His wife is attending for the very first time, having heard a great deal about it. So we can imagine that the audience of 1607 must have been well tuned-in to the glance towards *Macbeth*, written only a year earlier, when Jasper the resourceful page pretends to be his own ghost in order to prompt guilt in his master:

> *Enter Merchant, solus*
> MERCHANT   I will have no great store of company at the wedding: a couple of neighbours and their wives, and we will have a capon in stewed broth, with marrow, and a good peece of beef, stuck with rosemary.
> *Enter Jasper, his face mealed*
> JASPER   Forbear thy pains, fond man, it is too late.
> MERCHANT   Heaven bless me! Jasper?

JASPER   Ay, I am his ghost
  Whom thou hast injured for his constant love.
  Fond worldly wretch, who dost not understand
  In death that true hearts cannot parted be.
  [...]
                              I will visit thee
  With ghastly looks, and put into thy mind
  The great offences which thou didst to me.
  When thou art at thy table with thy friends,
  Merry in heart and filled with swelling wine,
  I'll come in midst of all thy pride and mirth,
  Invisible to all men but thyself,
  And whisper such a sad tale in thine ear,
  Shall make thee let the cup fall from thy hand,
  And stand as mute and pale as death itself.[10]

Jasper has used a theatrical technique to make himself appear ghostly—he appears with his face 'mealed', covered in flour. He then claims to have been killed by a broken heart, caused by the Merchant's refusal to let him marry his daughter, and threatens to haunt him. The scene that is conjured up is exactly that found in *Macbeth*, where the usurping King is terrified by an apparition that only he can see, in front of his guests. *The Knight of the Burning Pestle* is full of references to recent stage successes, often not by Shakespeare. Many of these are part of a satire of popular theatrical taste, especially its enthusiasm for swashbuckling romances, but the Banquo revival does not fit in with this. Jasper imagines a scene that is a pale reflection of the original, but in doing so the play pays tribute to *Macbeth*. Perhaps there is a dig at the strain put on theatrical resources and audience credulity by the creation of a ghost by judicious use of flour and fake blood. Nevertheless the Shakespearian scene is not made to seem like something memorable only for the weaker-minded among his audience.

Fletcher writes a number of plays that act as creative commentaries on Shakespeare. The only true sequel among them continues the story of *The Taming of the Shrew*. In continuing this story *The Woman's Prize; or The Tamer Tamed* actually overturns many of the assumptions of its predecessor and starts abruptly with the death of Kate, and hence a brisk loss of all that was won before. Fletcher has Petruchio marry a woman, Maria, who gives him a terrible time. The opening of the play sees a revealing negotiation with its forerunner, as continuity is established—these two observers have no idea of the personality of Petruchio's new wife:

MOROSE   I'll assure ye,
   I hold him a good man.
SOPHOCLES   Yes sure a wealthy,
   But whether a good woman's man, is doubtful.
TRANIO   Would 'twere no worse.
MOROSE   What though his other wife,
   Out of her most abundant stubbornness,
   Out of her daily hue and cries upon him,
   For sure she was a rebel, turned his temper,
   And forced him blow as high as she? Dost follow
   He must retain that long since buried tempest,
   To this soft maid?
   [...]
TRANIO   For yet the bare remembrance of his first wife
   (I tell ye on my knowledge, and a truth too)
   Will make him start in's sleep, and very often
   Cry out for cudgels, colstaves, any thing;
   Hiding his breeches, out of fear her ghost
   Should walk, and wear 'em yet. Since his first marriage,
   He is no more the still Petruchio,
   Than I am Babylon.[11]

The matter of *The Taming of the Shrew* is depicted as a 'bare remembrance' that will haunt the action of the new play. Yet it has also had a transformative effect on the central characters—these observers deem him 'no more the still Petruchio' after all his earlier antics. So Fletcher's play establishes its novelty and its imaginative space in relation to the first instalment of the story, but it also allows itself to be marked by what happened there. As it turns out the temper that will dominate the new play (as the title makes plain) is not the one they fear. So the first scene is still, in a way, in the mode of the previous play. In the end Petruchio feigns death in order to win his wife back—something that could be read as a final exploration of the relationship between the new play and the old. At the point of crisis the central characters, one from the old play and one entirely from the new, are almost parted, and the inherited figure appears dead. The audience is confronted with a severed bond between Fletcher and Shakespeare. Reconciliation of husband and wife, and of the two plays, follows.

The Woman's Prize; or The Tamer Tamed starts with a dramatic tension between Fletcher and Shakespeare that appears bounded by mutual respect and an attempt to build a separate body of work without offending the pre-existing Shakespearian corpus. Instead, connections and supplementary pathways are created. It starts with a marriage rather than a funeral. The harmony of the interaction between the two writers is evident not only in constructive exchange: it is actually most manifest in the benign demeanour of moments of point-scoring between Fletcher and Shakespeare. Fletcher's manoeuvres around the fringes of *The Tempest* suggest a deep fascination for, and interest in, that play—partly because its motifs recur, and partly because Fletcher makes respectful fun of the play's quirks. In *The Two Noble Kinsmen* Fletcher is usually credited with the Jailer's Daughter scenes, and in one of them there seems to be a gentle parody of the storm scene in *The Tempest*, a scene to which Fletcher returns elsewhere:

> DAUGHTER   You are master of a ship?
> JAILER   Yes.
> DAUGHTER   Where's your compass?
> JAILER   Here.
> DAUGHTER   Set it to th' north.
>   And now direct your course to th' wood where Palamon
>   Lies longing for me. For the tackling,
>   Let me alone. Come, weigh, my hearts, cheerly all.
>   Uff, uff, uff! 'Tis up. The wind's fair. Top the bowline.
>   Out with the mainsail! Where's your whistle, master?
> BROTHER   Let's get her in.
> JAILER   Up to the top, boy!
> BROTHER   Where's the pilot?
> FIRST FRIEND   Here.
> DAUGHTER   What kenn'st thou?
> SECOND FRIEND   A fair wood.
> DAUGHTER   Bear for it, master.
>   Tack about!

> (4.1.140–50)

It is of interest that the imitative storm scene comes in Fletcher's part of the play, but it would be wrong to overstress his ownership of it, and thereby to imply that Shakespeare might not have welcomed its humour. In her madness the Jailer's Daughter is convinced that she is on a boat and that she can sail to a wood, accompanied by her crew of friends and relations. She sets a nautical tone when she urges on 'my hearts', and then parallels the storm scene in *The Tempest* by adopting technical vocabulary and verbal expressions of urgency and effort; her retinue joins in half-heartedly. The scene challenges the famous opening of *The Tempest* in its technique, then, but most of all in its effect. As has already been discussed, the Shakespearian storm employs powerful realistic strategies in order to create a stark contrast with the suspicion one might have about appearances, given Prospero's powers as an illusionist:

> MASTER   Good, speak to th' mariners. Fall to't yarely, or we run ourselves aground. Bestir, bestir!   *Exit*
>> *Enter Mariners*
>
> BOATSWAIN   Heigh, my hearts! Cheerly, cheerly, my hearts! Yare, yare! Take in the topsail! Tend to th' Master's whistle!—Blow till thou burst thy wind, if room enough.
> [...]
> BOATSWAIN   Down with the topmast! Yare! Lower, lower! Bring her to try wi'th' main-course!
>> *A cry within*
>
> A plague upon this howling! They are louder than the weather, or our office.
> [...]
> BOATSWAIN   Lay her a-hold, a-hold! Set her two courses! Off to sea again! Lay her off!
>> *Enter Mariners, wet*
>
> MARINERS   All lost! To prayers, to prayers! All lost! [*Exeunt Mariners*]
> [...]
>> *A confused noise within*
>
> MARINERS (*within*)   Mercy on us!
> We split, we split! Farewell, my wife and children!
> Farewell, brother! We split, we split, we split!
>
> (1.1.3–7, 33–6, 47–9, 57–9.)

It is highly unusual to be so specific about the components of an offstage noise, as in the last three lines here—evidently it was important to bring out the diversity of the thoughts of people in crisis. The speech prefix 'Mariners' is not there in the Folio text, so the lines are in effect a stage direction with an unusual level of detail. This was probably added to the manuscript by the scribe Ralph Crane, rather than being Shakespeare's own contribution. Even so, it suggests that there was something special about the staging of the individual voices found within this 'confused noise'. As was discussed in Chapter 2, Shakespeare features onstage reactions to the spectacles being presented; soon afterwards there is Miranda's immediate response to the storm, swept up in its drama but tellingly appreciating it almost as a drama. In *The Two Noble Kinsmen* an ironic glance is sent towards both these reactions because its storm is appreciated candidly by a mad woman and bemusedly by some game but unwilling onlookers-turned-participants. The experimental analysis of how drama interacts with its audience that lies behind Shakespeare's scene is recast in a slightly farcical form. The ineptitude of Fletcher's characters' version ensures that the negotiation includes its share of tribute, since the original is so much more effective. The tragic poignancy of the Jailer's Daughter herself prevents the scene appearing too self-satisfied.

This is just one snapshot of *The Two Noble Kinsmen* and its kind of collaboration. Charles Frey and Donald Hedrick have both written about how this play actually takes duality of authorship into its thematic network alongside its other doublings.[12] It is a play about close friends which is written by close colleagues; it allows conflict to flourish, and one of the partners leaves the other to continue life and work. Fletcher seems to have felt able and authorized to pay a humorous and slightly double-edged tribute to Shakespeare. *The Sea Voyage* displays the longer term persistence of Fletcher's interest in *The Tempest*. In it many familiar aspects of plot and theme are replayed—the shipwreck, the encounter with island-dwellers, a lost wife rediscovered, the social mixture, and old scores. It starts with a storm, a more straightforward homage to Shakespeare than the Jailer's Daughter's storm in *The Two Noble Kinsmen*:

> [*A Tempest, Thunder and Lightning.*
> *Enter Master and two Sailors*
> MASTER Lay her aloof, the sea grows dangerous.
> How it spits against the clouds, how it capers,
> And how the fiery element frights it back!
> There be devils dancing in the air, I think.

I saw a dolphin hang i'th' horns of the moon,
Shot from a wave. Hey day, hey day,
How she kicks and jerks!
Down with the main mast, lay her at hull,
Furl up all her linens, and let her ride it out.
FIRST SAILOR   She'll never brook it, Master.
She's so deep laden, that she'll bulge.
[...]
FIRST SAILOR   Stand in, stand in, we are all lost else, lost and perished!
MASTER   Steer her a-starboard there!
SECOND SAILOR   Bear in with all the sail we can! See, Master,
See, what a clap of thunder there is,
What a face of heaven, how dreadfully it looks?
MASTER   Thou rascal, thou fearful rogue, thou hast been praying!
I see't in thy face, thou hast been mumbling!
When we are split, you slave—is this a time
To discourage our friends with your cold orisons?
Call up the boatswain! How it storms! holla![13]

In addition to the stress and strain, and the technical terms, this version picks up the contention between the strugglers that characterizes the scene in *The Tempest*. The class conflict in Shakespeare is clearer, as the courtly passengers clash with the Boatswain. Under extreme conditions Gonzalo, for example, has to face up to his complete distrust in the people to whom he has given his safety. In Fletcher the contention is within the crew, as the Master lambasts the discord in his inferiors. Nevertheless the candid and powerful exposure of solidarity crumbling under pressure is shared. The reference back to *The Tempest* is clear and again it is handled with tact—though overall the play is more robustly comic than Shakespeare's. Many things in the ensuing play must be read in relation to their precedents, but there is not really a sense that the competition is aimed at the disadvantage of Shakespeare.

The storm and shipwreck scene is followed by the reactions of Sebastian and Nicusa, an uncle and nephew who have been marooned on the island for many years. Their status as onlookers parallels the perspectives of Prospero and Miranda. It may be significant that the relationship between Sebastian and Nicusa is one step less direct, as if the imitation must register itself in a lower degree of closeness. In addition, these observers lack the sense of control over events that

Prospero and (to a lesser extent) Miranda have. So the irony gained from the Fletcherian repetition is balanced by the lack of irony derived from having a magician watching the effects of his own illusion. When the shipboard characters of *The Sea Voyage* arrive on the island and meet its inhabitants, they find them more as Calibans:

> AMINTA   But ha! What things are these,
> > *Enter Sebastian and Nicusa*
>   Are they human creatures?
> TIBALT   I have heard of sea-calves.
> ALBERT   No shadows, sure, they have legs and arms.
> TIBALT   They hang but lightly on, though.
>
>   (1.4.98–101)

Here the comical misrecognition of humans as beasts ('sea-calves') recalls Stefano and Trinculo encountering Caliban. In addition, the speculation about their status as 'shadows' recalls the spirits of Prospero's island rather than its human slave. Fletcher squeezes two features of *The Tempest* into close proximity. Yet again the affiliation with Shakespeare is made clear, and Fletcher has the confidence to incorporate the Shakespearian material and move beyond it, while also remaining genial and deferent in relation to his predecessor.

Henry VIII is a special example of 'incorporation', a collaborative play with a design that is both single and multiple, telling the story of one King's reign through several key episodes. As a dramatic body, a corpus in five acts, it is held together (like any body) by some flexible joints. The ease and energy of these connections is elegant testimony to the quality of this collaboration. They are the articulations of the play's structure also in the sense that sometimes they lay open the fact that the play is an exchange between writers as well as a series of episodes. The two gentlemen who describe the coronation procession of Queen Anne, for example, speak like characters, authors, and audience:

> *Enter the two Gentlemen meeting one another. The first holds a paper*
> FIRST GENTLEMAN   You're well met once again.
> SECOND GENTLEMAN   So are you.
> FIRST GENTLEMAN   You come to take your stand here and behold
>   The Lady Anne pass from her coronation?
> SECOND GENTLEMAN   'Tis all my business. At our last encounter
>   The Duke of Buckingham came from his trial.

FIRST GENTLEMAN   'Tis very true. But that time offered sorrow,
This, general joy.
SECOND GENTLEMAN
                    'Tis well. The citizens,
I am sure, have shown at full their royal minds—
As, let 'em have their rights, they are ever forward—
In celebration of this day with shows,
Pageants, and sights of honour.
FIRST GENTLEMAN   Never greater,
Nor, I'll assure you, better taken, sir.
SECOND GENTLEMAN   May I be so bold to ask what that contains,
That paper in your hand?
FIRST GENTLEMAN   Yes, 'tis the list
Of those that claim their offices this day
By custom of the coronation.
The Duke of Suffolk is the first, and claims
To be High Steward; next, the Duke of Norfolk,
He to be Earl Marshal. You may read the rest.
       He gives him the paper
SECOND GENTLEMAN   I thank you, sir. Had I not known those
            customs,
I should have been beholden to your paper.
But I beseech you, what's become of Katherine,
The Princess Dowager? How goes her business?

                                        (4.1.1–23)

This exchange comes, if Vickers and others are right in their allocation
of scenes, as Fletcher takes over from Shakespeare. At the beginning
the two characters work through the hinged connection between
episodes by means of a series of dualities—this time/last time, sor-
row/joy. The second gentleman's query as to what is contained in
the paper held by the first gentleman opens up the possibility for a
stylish self-conscious gesture. The paper could become a metaphor
for dual authorship, a physical representation of the transference of
episodic authority from one author to another. (It could do other
things too, such as highlighting the authority of the chronicle source
in providing details.) However, this is quickly overturned when the
second gentleman turns out to have been equipped with the same
information: 'Had I not known those customs, | I should have been
beholden to your paper.' What could have divided the two authors

turns out to be shared. The exchange takes a further turn when the second gentleman relinquishes authority again in asking for news about Katherine, thus initiating the sequence of action preceding her death. The two gentlemen are an eloquent representation of the sinuous, harmonious relationship between Shakespeare and Fletcher.

Henry VIII is a play that revels in those moments where the organization of action becomes an issue. Because it does not have a linear narrative the question of access—what the audience will see, what it should see, what it could see—becomes acute. Late in the play a Porter and the Lord Chamberlain discuss the crowd gathered in anticipation of the arrival of the new baby Princess Elizabeth:

> *Noise and tumult within. Enter Porter [with rushes]*
> *and his man [with a broken cudgel]*
> PORTER   You'll leave your noise anon, ye rascals. Do you take
> The court for Paris Garden, ye rude slaves?
> Leave your gaping.
> [...]
> PORTER   These are the youths that thunder at a playhouse, and fight
> for bitten apples, that no audience but the tribulation of Tower Hill
> or the limbs of Limehouse, their dear brothers, are able to endure. I
> have some of 'em in *limbo patrum*, and there they are like to dance
> these three days, besides the running banquet of two beadles that is to
> come.
> *Enter the Lord Chamberlain*
> LORD CHAMBERLAIN   Mercy o' me, what a multitude are here!
> They grow still, too—from all parts they are coming,
> As if we kept a fair here! Where are these porters,
> These lazy knaves? (*To the Porter and his man*) You've made a fine
> hand, fellows!
> There's a trim rabble let in—are all these
> Your faithful friends o'th' suburbs? We shall have
> Great store of room, no doubt, left for the ladies
> When they pass back from the christening!

(5.3.1–3, 58–72)

The Porter is explicit that the assembled crowd resembles an audience at the theatre. This is the most pointed of the plethora of London references, a range of locations neatly categorized by the noble Lord Chamberlain as the haunts of 'your faithful friends o'th' suburbs'.

These two little moments both feature people within the play keeping back the press of a crowd. This is the opposite of the actors' mission; they want to attract an audience. The play comically advertises the attractiveness of its subject-matter by attempting to restrain internal enthusiasm. At this point the collaboration is not on the surface, but confident exchanges and supple organization are typical of the Shakespeare–Fletcher method.

The interaction between them is not only seen in their collaborations or indeed in those plays with debts to previous work. Fletcher's reputation as a dramatist rests not least on his tragicomedies, *Philaster* and *A King and No King*, both genuinely innovative and unusual dramas. There are still fascinating negotiations with Shakespeare, but there are also some fundamental differences between their works that are very instructive about late Shakespeare. *Philaster* revisits elements of *Hamlet*, *Othello*, *Twelfth Night*, and others, but what is perhaps most interesting is its relationship with *Cymbeline*.[14] Critics have tied themselves in knots working out which came first, in order to establish who is imitating whom. However, it may be most productive to look at how the parallels between the two plays may be evidence of a new kind of drama being produced in a corporate fashion by the leading dramatists of the King's Men at the same time. There are specific comparisons between the plots of *Cymbeline* and *Philaster*, such as the strand where in both plays women act as the pages of their unwitting loves. Alongside these there are parallels in tone and texture of the tragicomedy that establish the closeness of the two plays:

> *Enter Trasiline with Philaster, Arathusa, Bellario, in a robe and garland*
> KING　How now, what masque is this?
> BELLARIO　Right royal Sir, I should
> 　　Sing you an epithalamion of these lovers,
> 　　But having lost my best airs with my fortunes,
> 　　And wanting a celestial harp to strike
> 　　This blessed union on, thus in glad story
> 　　I give you all. These two fair cedar branches,
> 　　The noblest of the mountain where they grew
> 　　Straightest and tallest, under whose still shades
> 　　The worthier beasts have made their lairs, and slept
> 　　Free from the fervour of the Sirian star
> 　　And the fell thunder-stroke, free from the clouds,
> 　　When they were big with humour, and delivered

> In thousand spouts, their issues to the earth:
> O there was none but silent quiet there![15]

This moment in *Philaster* strikes numerous chords with late Shakespeare. The reference to the masque form, the idea of a 'celestial harp' striking for a 'blessed union', the 'cedar branches' (specific to *Cymbeline*), the spouting clouds, and the awestruck style—all these things demonstrate the connection between this play and contemporary developments in Shakespeare. It is not vital to determine whether Fletcher is responding to Shakespeare or helping forge something new, but the possibility of the latter is a useful corrective to a single-mindedly author-based vision of the characteristics of late Shakespeare.

After discussing points of intersection between Fletcher and Shakespeare in his tragicomedies, it is necessary to consider an important and instructive difference. Shakespeare rarely surprises his audiences with unforeseen plot-twists. There are half-truths and uncertainties, as with Helena's plots in *All's Well That Ends Well*; there are the shocks and reversals that fit with the unfolding of a tragic plot; but there are very few places where the action of a play contravenes what amount to previously accepted facts. Perhaps the only real examples are Hermione's statue-scene in *The Winter's Tale* and the appearance of Aemilia in *The Comedy of Errors*—an early play with other romance qualities, as was briefly mentioned in Chapter 1. To some extent Hermione's transformation is a genuine surprise, but Apollo's prophecy paves the way for something to happen, and the audience must be expecting a climax. In addition, there is the strange problem with interpreting Shakespeare, more than with most authors, that many members of the audience, and readers too, know already that the statue will come to life. Like the bear of 3.3, it can be a novelty that people prepare themselves for in advance. So there is nothing in Shakespeare quite like the complete reversals found in Fletcher and other writers. Something like the miraculous conversion of the evil Duke in *As You Like It* is not quite the same: this is a marginal occurrence in comparison. *The Winter's Tale* would be a tragicomedy even without Hermione's return, but this is certainly not true of *Philaster*. There the hero suspects Arathusa of infidelity with his page Bellario, and everything looks bleak until Bellario reveals himself to be Euphrasia, daughter to Dion. The audience, perhaps, must be waiting for something to happen in very general terms, but this is a surprise means of overcoming Philaster's groundless suspicion:

> DION   O 'tis just, 'tis she,
> Now I do know thee. O, that thou hadst died
> And I had never seen thee, nor my shame.
> How shall I own thee, shall this tongue of mine
> E'er call thee daughter more?
> BELLARIO   Would I had died indeed! I wish it too,
> And so must have done by vow, ere published
> What I have told, but that there was no means
> To hide it longer. Yet I joy in this,
> The princess is all clear.
>
>   (5.5.113–22)

The hidden fact, once it has come out, changes everything and the audience has not been prepared for it.[16] Dion and 'Bellario' both come across as deeply moved in their speeches. The latter in particular is in a state of confusion, uncertain of anything except the immediate plot crisis her revelation solves. It is a great dramatic coup: the key question that emerges is why Shakespeare should avoid such coups.

Before going into that question, it is worth noting the equivalent moment in *A King and No King*. There King Arbaces is in love with his sister Panthaea—which would be a huge problem, except she is not his sister. The audience finds this out at the same time as the King: the play's time-frame is not changed thereby (the joyful and disastrous endings would have happened at the same critical point) but the representation and ordering of time in the play are complicated. As Gobrius approaches the moment at which he must reveal his extraordinary knowledge (that he is the actual father of the King, who is therefore no King) he expresses a sense of unfolding time:

> GOBRIUS   There is the king,
> Now it is ripe.
> [...]
> GOBRIUS   [*Aside*] Now is the time. Hear me but speak.
> [...]
> GOBRIUS   Sir, you shall know your sins before you do 'em:
> If you kill me—
> ARBACES   I will not stay then.

GOBRIUS   Know
You kill your father.[17]

Soon after the King seems to press for more proof of this news, but
he is assuaged by a plain reassurance. The dramatic necessity of the
revealed facts, and the benefit bestowed on him thereby, means he
does not linger long to wait for details:

ARBACES   But can you prove this?
GOBRIUS   If you will give consent—
Else who dare go about it?
ARBACES   Give consent?
Why I will have them all that know it racked
To get this from 'em. All that waits without
Come in, whate'er you be, come in, and be
Partakers of my joy.
            Enter Mardonius, Bessus, and others
            O, you are welcome.
Mardonius, the best news!—Nay, draw no nearer.
They all shall hear it: I am found no King!

(5.4.257–64)

A King and No King comes close to tragic crisis: Arbaces is truly
torn between his duty and the passion he thinks is incestuous. The
outcome remains unclear until a fact of which the audience has little
inkling—until Gobrius begins to boil over—emerges in the nick of
time. Verna Foster has suggested a fundamental contrast between
the texture of surprise in Fletcher, compared with *The Winter's Tale*,
where the wondrous event emerges more naturally from the rest of
the play: 'The naturalness of the ending when it comes, combined
with our tentative and incomplete sense of Hermione's loss, creates the
impression that we have always known (not that we *should* have known
if we had only picked up on the clues as in Fletcherian tragicomedy,
but that we *have known*) that Hermione was still alive.'[18] This seems
right, even if it is difficult to corroborate with specific textual evidence.
Even when contriving scenes of true amazement, Shakespeare does
not entirely remove the audience from the impression of knowledge,
even if he does deny knowledge itself.
    The dynamics of tragicomedy and romance are clearly import-
ant in the work of Shakespeare, of Fletcher, and in collaborations

between Fletcher and Shakespeare. Alongside, and partly in conflict with, interest in the characteristics of Shakespeare's late work,
there is also a need to recognize how other dramatists, Fletcher in
particular, were sharing and participating in the same thematic and
generic manoeuvres. Late Shakespeare, then, can partly be seen as
his participation in a wider cultural tendency. The contrasts between
Fletcher and Shakespeare justify the word 'partly'. It becomes all the
more necessary to consider why so much of what is essential to the
happy endings of Shakespearian romance (and his drama in general)
is meticulously prepared. Why does Shakespeare avoid the surprise
coups that could have added a new kind of animation to his dramatic
conclusions? The Introduction has already set out the key reason to
be advanced here, which is that Shakespeare aims to foster irony and
multiple layers to contemplate, rather than providing single-layered
wonders to amaze. This is of general importance in Shakespeare, who
seems to miss no opportunity to engage his audience or readers in
thought. It is also of specific importance in his late work, because
in these plays Shakespeare attempts a serious and profound balance,
both sceptical and ironic, between the espousal of powerful ideas, and
a necessary step back from any false certainties. As will be seen in
the next chapter, Shakespeare also revisits themes and scenes from his
earlier work and then replays them: the energy and tension of the earlier plays is partly converted into irony, partly redirected towards the
next stage of particular characters' journeys. In relation to Fletcher's
surprises, Shakespeare contrasts because he avoids a technique that
denies an ironic perspective. The transformation of Hermione could
be a recognition of, and experiment in, the potential for surprising
romance scenes revealed in his colleague's work. Of course, Fletcher
may well be varying from Shakespeare rather than vice versa. It is a
central difference between them that adds a layer to the interaction
between the two writers, one which is unusually rich and genuinely
cooperative.

Shakespeare, Early and Late

> That she is living,
> Were it but told you, should be hooted at
> Like an old tale. But it appears she lives,
> Though yet she speak not.
>
> (*The Winter's Tale*, 5.3.116–19)

As was explored in an earlier chapter, Shakespeare sharpens his audience's sense of what the word 'appears' may offer. This story is incredible to the ear, but as a visual spectacle it transcends seeming and overcomes objections. In this chapter the focus shifts away from the technique and value of representation and towards the 'old tales' that are being re-presented. *Pericles* is based on the story of Apollonius of Tyre as retold in Lawrence Twyne's *Pattern of Painful Adventures*, originally published in 1576 and reprinted in 1607. *The Winter's Tale* has as its main source Robert Greene's *Pandosto* (1588, reprinted several times in the next two decades). So Shakespeare is working with the material of 'old tales' of the 1570s and 1580s, and he is capitalizing on more recent revivals. It is worth remembering that *Pericles* incorporates a further layer of oldness in its tale by using the medieval poet Gower as a chorus. In contrast, *The Tempest* has no source as such but is often connected with the narrative of a New World shipwreck in 1609.[1] Nevertheless it is notable that in the late plays innovation is based on recapitulation. In particular, this chapter will centre on the ways in which Shakespeare revisits and revises the interests of his earlier works in his final plays. When thematic affinities are evident it is often clear that Shakespeare is not repeating himself on the same terms. The focus of his drama has shifted, with the effect that the things that mattered most in earlier plays no longer seem so central, as richer contexts are found.

The Two Gentlemen of Verona is a very early play indeed—probably first performed as early as 1590, at the very beginning of Shakespeare's career. It has a great deal in common with *The Two Noble Kinsmen*, their affinity captured in their titles. The earlier story's two gentlemen are Proteus and Valentine, whose friendship is sorely tested by a conflict over love. Proteus, changeable as befits his name, betrays and plots against his friend for love of Silvia:

> Already have I been false to Valentine,
> And now I must be as unjust to Thurio.
> Under the colour of commending him
> I have access my own love to prefer.
> But Silvia is too fair, too true, too holy
> To be corrupted with my worthless gifts.
> When I protest true loyalty to her
> She twits me with my falsehood to my friend.
> When to her beauty I commend my vows
> She bids me think how I have been forsworn
> In breaking faith with Julia, whom I loved.
> And notwithstanding all her sudden quips,
> The least whereof would quell a lover's hope,
> Yet, spaniel-like, the more she spurns my love,
> The more it grows, and fawneth on her still.
>
> (4.2.1–15)

Thurio is yet another competitor in love—the local suitor who represents a conventional outlet for rivalry. The perversity of passion means that Proteus's faithlessness (that to his friend comes before that to his previous lover) becomes part of the taunting, but only whets his appetite further. Under the test of love, friendship explodes. It is reconstituted at the end of the play, when at the extreme of their hatred, they remember themselves:

> VALENTINE   Thou common friend, that's without faith or love,
> For such is a friend now. Treacherous man,
> Thou hast beguiled my hopes! Naught but mine eye
> Could have persuaded me. Now I dare not say
> I have one friend alive. Thou wouldst disprove me.
> Who should be trusted, when one's right hand

> Is perjured to the bosom? Proteus,
> I am sorry I must never trust thee more,
> But count the world a stranger for thy sake.
> The private wound is deepest. O time most accursed,
> 'Mongst all foes that a friend should be the worst!
> PROTEUS   My shame and guilt confounds me.
> Forgive me, Valentine. If hearty sorrow
> Be a sufficient ransom for offence,
> I tender't here. I do as truly suffer
> As e'er I did commit.
> VALENTINE   Then I am paid,
> And once again I do receive thee honest.
> Who by repentance is not satisfied
> Is nor of heaven nor earth. For these are pleased;
> By penitence th' Eternal's wrath's appeased.
> And that my love may appear plain and free,
> All that was mine in Silvia I give thee.

$$(5.4.62-83)$$

Yet it is Valentine whose love for Silvia wins in the end: Proteus, after moving himself almost entirely beyond redemption, recovers his love for Julia. These changes are so abrupt that they strain even comedy's rules. Proteus's recent threats of rape against Silvia add a further sharp note to assuage an audience's admiration of Valentine's generosity. The show of remorse is convincing but Valentine's posturing seems overblown—especially when he likens himself to merciful God. The play's comic atmosphere ebbs and flows with the currents of the two heroes' emotions—their names, representative of change and love, reflect their embodiment of the play's central themes. Its capriciousness and strangeness reflect a full investment in the changeable and energetic youths.

Things are rather different in *The Two Noble Kinsmen*. This is another 'old tale', derived from Chaucer's *Knight's Tale*. In *The Two Noble Kinsmen* love and friendship are again in conflict.[2] The crucial difference is that, while the play tracks the emotional dynamics of the heroes Palamon and Arcite, it does not invest fully in them. In the earlier comedy the whole structure of the play was involved in the ebb and flow of friendship, but in his collaboration with Fletcher Shakespeare keeps a different framework in view. The crisis of friendship starts when the two friends, in prison, see Emilia:

PALAMON   I that first saw her, I that took possession
     First with mine eye of all those beauties
     In her revealed to mankind. If thou lov'st her,
     Or entertain'st a hope to blast my wishes,
     Thou art a traitor, Arcite, and a fellow
     False as thy title to her. Friendship, blood,
     And all the ties between us I disclaim,
     If thou once think upon her.
ARCITE   Yes, I love her—
     And if the lives of all my name lay on it,
     I must do so. I love her with my soul—
     If that will lose ye, farewell, Palamon!
     I say again,
     I love her, and in loving her maintain
     I am as worthy and as free a lover,
     And have as just a title to her beauty,
     As any Palamon, or any living
     That is a man's son.

(2.2.170–86)

Before the moment of discovery Palamon and Arcite had been expressing just how happy they were to be on their own together. Their improbable intensity sets up the inevitable interruption in a rather formulaic way. At this point the quarrel is absurd for its futility. When fate takes a hand and they get free the quarrel's absurdity is different—then it is the formulaic absoluteness of the division that strains credibility. Their emotions do not define the structure of the play, however; instead it is the force of the unfolding plot that keeps things under greater control and places a bit of distance between the audience and the characters.

Nevertheless the crisis of friendship in *The Two Noble Kinsmen* involves moments that are more moving than anything in *The Two Gentlemen of Verona* partly because the tribulations of the central characters are not displayed in full focus. The scene where the two arm one another, as they have many times before, has already been mentioned as an example of Shakespeare's interest in intense friendship and its effects. Its pathos cannot be doubted, but the audience's interaction with that pathos is what matters most here. While *The Two Gentlemen of Verona* plays fast and loose with its psychological portraits, the struggles of friendship, young and shallow though they may be, are centrally at issue in the audience's experience of the play. In *The Two Noble Kinsmen* the audience can to some extent see round the pathos towards a different source of value. So there is a kind of detachment in the experience of the moving scene:

> ARCITE   Will you fight bare-armed?
> PALAMON   We shall be the nimbler.
> ARCITE   But use your gauntlets, though—those are o'th' least.
>   Prithee take mine, good cousin.
> PALAMON   Thank you, Arcite.
>   How do I look? Am I fall'n much away?
> ARCITE   Faith, very little—love has used you kindly.
> PALAMON   I'll warrant thee, I'll strike home.
> ARCITE   Do, and spare not—
>   I'll give you cause, sweet cousin.
> PALAMON   Now to you, sir.
>   *Palamon arms Arcite*
>   Methinks this armour's very like that, Arcite,
>   Thou wor'st that day the three kings fell, but lighter.
>
>   (3.6.63–71)

There are some remarkable shared feelings and gestures here, and the reminiscence goes on for a while longer. Before this Arcite ruefully reflects on how far he has fallen ('to say true, I stole it', line 55), and this is a small version of the huge rueful reflection to which this scene is subject. There are moments of tenderness and generosity ('Prithee take mine'), self-doubt and comfort ('How do I look?' ... 'Love has used you kindly'), and finally, a shared memory: 'Methinks this armour's very like that, Arcite, | Thou wor'st that day the three kings fell, but lighter.' Thus the scene taps into such reserves of poignancy that an audience might rebel against it as a kind of travesty. The tension of love and friendship in *The Two Gentlemen of Verona* was acute and quick to alter, whereas in *The Two Noble Kinsmen* it is absolute and schematic. However, it is also curiously undramatic—the unfolding of the plot at that level is not the key process of the play. Instead the focus is on the larger structure towards which the contention of love and friendship is leading—the redemptive structure of romance.

At the end of *The Two Noble Kinsmen* the two friends are reconciled in a very different spirit from *The Two Gentlemen of Verona*. In the earlier play the energy was derived from the emotional complexity of the reunion under such strained circumstances. In the later play the human actions are in harmony with a miraculous divine solution and the fulfilment of an impossible plot. Both heroes have their prayers answered when the winner of the battle (Arcite) does not live long enough to enjoy the spoils:

> PALAMON   O miserable end of our alliance!
> The gods are mighty. Arcite, if thy heart,
> Thy worthy manly heart, be yet unbroken,
> Give me thy last words. I am Palamon,
> One that yet loves thee dying.
> ARCITE   Take Emilia,
> And with her all the world's joy. Reach thy hand—
> Farewell—I have told my last hour. I was false,
> Yet never treacherous. Forgive me, cousin—
> One kiss from fair Emilia—(*they kiss*) 'tis done.
> Take her; I die.
>
> (5.6.86–95)

There is new pathos in the plot of faithless friends rediscovering one another, but this repeated plot is a way of guiding readers and audiences towards a meaning of a different kind. The friendship theme is not developed as the central process of the play—instead it is one layer of another process, in which the deepest providential forces of the play are at work. This shift of focus is in line with the characteristics of late Shakespeare observed in earlier chapters: the turn away from the central theme of friendship includes a hint of irony, but the irony does not disparage friendship in the play. The point is not to argue that Shakespearian romance is deeper or more capacious than his comedy or indeed his tragedy, just that in these plays the human dramas are played out in relation to a plot with a different shape and different priorities. This parallel plot—redemptive romance, discovery and rediscovery, a providential order—cannot be taken as a given: it is problematic and contested throughout. The really important thing this chapter has to offer is the thought that this novel direction arises in the midst of repetitions, and revisions, of earlier works.

A similar pattern can be observed in the versions of jealousy presented in *The Winter's Tale* and *Othello*. The earlier play explores the complexity and disorientation of powerful emotion, and the whole play is affected by the ramifications of the hero's struggle. The romance version of tragic jealousy also portrays the twisted psychology of the hero, but its role in the play is different. Tillyard argued that the late plays followed the tragic pattern but then had the imaginative scope to move beyond it.³ This model still has things to offer, but the example of jealousy shows that it is not so much a sequential pattern as a question of how much the tragic action creates a tragic world. In *Othello*, then, jealousy is portrayed spreading maliciously throughout the structure of the play:

> O, beware, my lord, of jealousy.
> It is the green-eyed monster which doth mock
> The meat it feeds on. That cuckold lives in bliss
> Who, certain of his fate, loves not his wronger.
> But O, what damnèd minutes tells he o'er
> Who dotes yet doubts, suspects yet fondly loves!
>
> (3.3.169–74)

174 fondly] strongly Q1; soundly F1.

The Oxford edition uses a word in the final line that is taken from neither of the variant original texts. The Quarto word 'strongly' creates an image of ardent, frenetic love in keeping with doting and doubting. Folio's 'soundly' is paradoxical, but could be sardonically rather than meaninglessly so, and thus effective in a rather different way. Iago is perhaps able to conjure up the conviction of the jealous lover. The Folio text is now usually thought of as a revised version of the play, which may give it extra authority. This may also validate the Oxford editors' decision to follow Knight in amending F to a more straightforward word—in manuscript 'fondly' and 'soundly' could easily have been confused. It represents a later stage of composition, and is thus privileged over Q ('strongly' there is an 'authorial alternative'), despite the possible need to rectify a problem in meaning.⁴ It is an interesting tangle which does not unravel into a clearly superior reading. In any version of this speech Iago is effective in manoeuvring Othello into the state of paranoia that he warns against, and he also helps plant anxiety in the play more broadly. The audience of *Othello* feels at times as if it is in a state of ineffectual vigilance, always alert to signs that it can do nothing about. In this respect the audience's situation mirrors that of the hero. In parallel, his stark assessment of the fragility of his mind feeds the audience's sense that the whole play is poised on the edge of horror:

> Perdition catch my soul
> But I do love thee, and when I love thee not,
> Chaos is come again.

(3.3.91–3)

Chaos is experienced as something imminent, and this feeling is pervasive. The atmosphere of Cyprus is suffused with turmoil, and the audience is more than just involved in the extremity and brittleness of Othello's reactions—the whole response to the play cannot escape these characteristics. Accordingly, when Desdemona appears it is very hard to avoid a repellent yet compelling feeling that she is veering towards wanton behaviour. So, amid the chaste environment of the 'Willow' scene, it is still hard to avoid wishing she would not participate at all in Emilia's banter:

EMILIA   Shall I go fetch your nightgown?
DESDEMONA   No. Unpin me here.
   This Lodovico is a proper man.
EMILIA   A very handsome man.
DESDEMONA   He speaks well.
EMILIA   I know a lady in Venice would have walked barefoot to
   Palestine for a touch of his nether lip.

(4.3.33–7)

Shakespeare is careful to make Desdemona blameless almost to the point of inertness here. The nudity in prospect is of the most innocent kind, and Emilia's praise of Lodovico (itself innocuous) is much more mildly echoed by Desdemona. Nevertheless the extent to which this play as a whole has been perverted by its central figure's distorted world-view comes through: it is very difficult to watch Desdemona without seeing her as Othello sees her.

In *The Winter's Tale* Leontes' jealous rage arises suddenly but its presentation discovers psychological depths akin to those in *Othello*. The king's emotions are self-generating, requiring little stimulus or endorsement from outside. When he tells Camillo about his wife's infidelity his rhetoric is coercive. Imperatives, questions, and aggressive parentheses all prevent the listener (whose inferior social position already limits him) from denying anything:

> Ha' you not seen, Camillo—
> But that's past doubt; you have, or your eye-glass
> Is thicker than a cuckold's horn—or heard—
> For, to a vision so apparent, rumour
> Cannot be mute—or thought—for cogitation
> Resides not in that man that does not think—
> My wife is slippery? If thou wilt confess—
> Or else be impudently negative
> To have nor eyes, nor ears, nor thought—then say
> My wife's a hobby-horse, deserves a name
> As rank as any flax-wench that puts to
> Before her troth-plight. Say't, and justify't.
>
> (1.2.269–80)

Leontes' jealousy turns in on itself, as Iago says it does, but the experience of the audience in relation to it is very different from that in *Othello*. In the tragic version the audience was tied up in the circle, but in the later romance it spectates upon the reflexive quality of jealousy from outside. This is complex, because whereas in *Othello* the audience has a seasoned kind of certainty that Desdemona is innocent, in *The Winter's Tale* its faith in Hermione must be mustered quickly and without much onstage corroboration. Nevertheless, viewers and readers are, relatively speaking, outside the boundaries of the world of jealousy in the play, however vivid it is. Of course, it matters that Leontes entirely repents of his earlier feelings in Act 3, rather than in Act 5. However, a difference of similar magnitude exists because the pervasiveness is evident but limited to the King himself:

> Is whispering nothing?
> Is leaning cheek to cheek? Is meeting noses?
> Kissing with inside lip? Stopping the career
> Of laughter with a sigh?—a note infallible
> Of breaking honesty. Horsing foot on foot?
> Skulking in corners? Wishing clocks more swift,
> Hours minutes, noon midnight? And all eyes
> Blind with the pin and web but theirs, theirs only,
> That would unseen be wicked? Is this nothing?
> Why then the world and all that's in't is nothing,
> The covering sky is nothing, Bohemia nothing,

My wife is nothing, nor nothing have these nothings
If this be nothing.

(1.2.286–99)

Jealousy here is as imaginative as it is in *Othello*, breeding words and
phrases with spontaneous fertility. As it does elsewhere in Shakespeare,
the word 'nothing' has more and more value even as it represents
absence and subtraction. However, the quality of its meaningfulness
is significantly different. In *Much Ado About Nothing* a variety of
meanings—the obvious negation, the phonetically linked 'noting',
and the innuendo in 'no-thing'—participate in the play's playfully
interconnected themes. However, it is in *King Lear* that it turns most
sharply as Cordelia and her father confront the word's weight in the
very first scene: 'nothing will come of nothing' (1.1.90), barks Lear,
but the play proves him wrong. In *The Winter's Tale* we are excluded
by, rather than involved in, these protestations: this world of 'nothing'
is Leontes' own, and his alone.

In the trial scene Hermione faces her husband's accusations with
extraordinary calm. She starts by making her case with poised desper-
ation, appealing for example to her lineage and her good character.
When these are quickly overcome by Leontes' conviction she gives a
candid, but still calm, account of her problem:

HERMIONE   You speak a language that I understand not.
  My life stands in the level of your dreams,
  Which I'll lay down.
LEONTES   Your actions are my 'dreams'.
  You had a bastard by Polixenes,
  And I but dreamed it.

(3.2.79–83)

The audience has become intensely involved in Leontes' dreams, but
not to the extent that they have begun to seem real in any way. When
Leontes first faces Apollo's oracle with defiance, and then asks for its
pardon, within the space of fifteen lines, the audience watches from
outside the stark ebb and flow of his mind:

  There is no truth at all i'th' oracle.
  The sessions shall proceed. This is mere falsehood. [...]

> Apollo, pardon
> My great profaneness 'gainst thine oracle.
>
> (3.2.139–40, 152–3)

It is not the case that having an awareness of the boundaries of Leontes' experience means that such experience is devalued. An awareness of boundaries of this kind could be called an ironic perspective, and the substance and constructive nature of late Shakespearian irony have already been asserted. The boundaries of the experience are in evidence and the play—this may be a characteristic one could associate with Shakespearian romance generally—guides the audience to consider things outside the personal stresses and strains of the action.

Something similar and perhaps even more schematic happens in *Cymbeline*. Jealousy takes over the whole of Posthumus's world, but not that of the play. His reaction to the news that he has apparently lost his wager with Giacomo causes a speech of violent generalizations. The audience cannot readily follow his extrapolation, as it is strained both in general and also as a feature of his character:

> For even to vice
> They are not constant, but are changing still
> One vice but of a minute old for one
> Not half so old as that. I'll write against them,
> Detest them, curse them, yet 'tis greater skill
> In a true hate to pray they have their will.
> The very devils cannot plague them better.
>
> (2.5.29–35)

These are hackneyed, standard misogynistic observations. They are not worthy of Posthumus, but this does not mean that their inclusion is an artistic fault. Rather, this passage of the play is unbalanced: only the providential restoration of right relations can end the discontinuities that result. Again the audience is not swept up in this, but instead we watch a series of scenes that undermine Posthumus's rhetoric yet more. In the next scene the focus of the play is on very different concerns: the King asks 'Now say, what would Augustus Caesar want with us?' (3.1.1). His eye is on high-level power politics. And then in the next scene the accusations of the jealous husband are given short shrift:

Enter Pisanio, reading of a letter

PISANIO   How? Of adultery? Wherefore write you not
What monster's her accuser? Leonatus,
O master, what a strange infection
Is fall'n into thy ear!

(3.2.1–4)

The emotions around jealousy are powerful and transforming but their effect is localized. Pisanio's loyalty to his master is easily overcome by his astonishment that the accusations could be so false. In *Cymbeline* jealousy and its expression play a relatively minor role, but it is still evident that tragic potential has been replaced by something else. There is still an emotionally scouring aspect to it, but it also takes place within an ostensibly providential system that precludes the full tragic unfolding of the jealousy plot.

Shakespeare's return to the jealousy plots and themes of earlier plays again sees him reviving the energies of earlier works but leaving some imaginative space around them. This is typical of the late plays' renegotiation of earlier themes—what were central concerns remain at the centre, but now the audience has additional distance from them. The plays' large romance structure prevails. This is true of other interactions with earlier plays. Two more examples will suffice here. One, an exchange between *The Tempest* and *A Midsummer Night's Dream*, probes the nature of drama. The first, however, reflects how the renegotiation in the late work can question the things at the core of the drama, without deflating them. *Henry VIII* explores the early Tudor period touched on in *Richard III*. Thus it encounters the development of the myth of unity to which later Tudors looked back:

> We will unite the white rose and the red.
> Smile, heaven, upon this fair conjunction,
> That long have frowned upon their enmity.
> What traitor hears me and says not 'Amen'?
> England hath long been mad, and scarred herself;
> The brother blindly shed the brother's blood;
> The father rashly slaughtered his own son;
> The son, compelled, been butcher to the sire;
> All this divided York and Lancaster,
> United in their dire division.
> O now let Richmond and Elizabeth,

> The true succeeders of each royal house,
> By God's fair ordinance conjoin together,
> And let their heirs—God, if his will be so—
> Enrich the time to come with smooth-faced peace,
> With smiling plenty, and fair prosperous days.
> Abate the edge of traitors, gracious Lord,
> That would reduce these bloody days again
> And make poor England weep forth streams of blood.
> Let them not live to taste this land's increase,
> That would with treason wound this fair land's peace.
> Now civil wounds are stopped; peace lives again.
> That she may long live here, God say 'Amen'.
>
> > (5.8.19–41)

This is Richmond's speech as he takes the crown of England. He announces and foretells an end to the turmoil of the Wars of the Roses. As well as looking back, he also looks forward in the subtle implication of the name 'Elizabeth'. It is shared by Henry VII's queen, a descendant of the house of York, and also by Shakespeare's own monarch. The tone here is satisfied and wishful at the same time: the 'smooth-faced peace' and 'fair prosperous days' might seem to have been achieved in the years since the accession of Henry VII, but it may have felt to an Elizabethan audience that these hopes had not been realized to such an ideal extent.

As has already been seen, *Henry VIII* finishes with a prophecy from Archbishop Cranmer that presents a passionate but very double-edged vision of the succeeding years. In this history play there is an additional layer of perspective on the featured story's role in grander narratives. This becomes distinctly ironic when an old lady reports to the King on the outcome of Queen Anne's labour. The play's dynastic aspect takes on a strange appearance:

> LOVELL (*within*) Come back! What mean you?
> OLD LADY   I'll not come back. The tidings that I bring
>   Will make my boldness manners. (*To the King*) Now good angels
>   Fly o'er thy royal head, and shade thy person
>   Under their blessèd wings.
> KING   Now by thy looks
>   I guess thy message. Is the Queen delivered?
>   Say, 'Ay, and of a boy.'

OLD LADY   Ay, ay, my liege,
  And of a lovely boy. The God of heaven
  Both now and ever bless her! 'Tis a girl
  Promises boys hereafter. Sir, your queen
  Desires your visitation, and to be
  Acquainted with this stranger. 'Tis as like you
  As cherry is to cherry.
KING   Lovell?—
LOVELL   Sir?
KING   Give her an hundred marks. I'll to the Queen.   *Exit*
OLD LADY   An hundred marks? By this light, I'll ha' more.
  An ordinary groom is for such payment.
  I will have more, or scold it out of him.
  Said I for this the girl was like to him? I'll
  Have more, or else unsay't; and now, while 'tis hot,
  I'll put it to the issue.

(5.1.158–77)

To some extent such representations of dynasties within plays must be double-edged. Within the scope of a play it is possible to localize an expression of hope for a given union or child. However, outside that scope, the nuances of misfortune that naturally attend every reign are ghostly presences. In *Richard III* this is partly true. Within the play the contrast between Richard III and his successor is absolute, though the audience might be aware of the victors' monopoly over truth, and indeed the violence and deceit of Henry VII's rule. In *Henry VIII* this goes a stage further: the hope that one might have for Princess Elizabeth has a localized aspect too—there are subsequent events and problems that must be forgotten. However, even within the play the tendentiousness of the optimistic view is in evidence. The old lady's self-serving and comical manipulation of the story allows the audience an additional perspective. She seeks to earn money by telling the King an untruth he wants to hear, that he has a son to carry on the dynasty. The end of the play only partly manages to elevate the daughter as a higher solution. In *Henry VIII*, then, there is yet another example of how the late plays create imaginative space around their plots.

In *A Midsummer Night's Dream* Theseus and Hippolyta have a highly important and nuanced exchange about the nature of the story they are told by the recently discovered lovers. They reflect, in fact, on the credibility of the rest of the action of the play, and of all dramatic action. The discussion is clearly one with ramifications beyond its context, but Shakespeare artfully measures its limits by unbalancing the argument. Hippolyta's response is short and truncated by the arrival of the lovers. Theseus's confidence is belied by the audience's experience of the drama, but his royal authority holds sway:

> HIPPOLYTA   'Tis strange, my Theseus, that these lovers speak of.
> THESEUS   More strange than true. I never may believe
>   These antique fables, nor these fairy toys.
>   Lovers and madmen have such seething brains,
>   Such shaping fantasies, that apprehend
>   More than cool reason ever comprehends.
>   The lunatic, the lover, and the poet
>   Are of imagination all compact.
>   One sees more devils than vast hell can hold:
>   That is the madman. The lover, all as frantic,
>   Sees Helen's beauty in a brow of Egypt.
>   The poet's eye, in a fine frenzy rolling,
>   Doth glance from heaven to earth, from earth to heaven,
>   And as imagination bodies forth
>   The forms of things unknown, the poet's pen
>   Turns them to shapes, and gives to airy nothing
>   A local habitation and a name.
>   Such tricks hath strong imagination
>   That if it would but apprehend some joy
>   It comprehends some bringer of that joy;
>   Or in the night, imagining some fear,
>   How easy is a bush supposed a bear!
> HIPPOLYTA   But all the story of the night told over,
>   And all their minds transfigured so together,
>   More witnesseth than fancy's images,
>   And grows to something of great constancy;
>   But howsoever, strange and admirable.

(5.1.1–27)

This speech hides within it a probable case of authorial revision, where evidence of lineation in the Quarto text (the first one printed) suggests that the lines concerning the poet were added at a second stage of composition.[5] If this is so, then the self-conscious gesture in aligning poets with lovers and madmen is a second thought, a discovery in the process of re-reading. Theseus denigrates the imagination as the source of false stories. Hippolyta is able to argue that collective experience might prove a greater reality in such stories: 'something of great constancy'. In this comedy such considerations are swept aside by the return to Athens of the lovers, and the performance by the mechanicals of the story of Pyramus and Thisbe. The debate is marginalized, despite it existing at what one might see as the primary level of the play, the daylight world of the court. However, it makes a crucial contribution by undermining the distinction between these levels of reality.

The Tempest looks back to *A Midsummer Night's Dream* in a number of ways. Both plays feature magic, and both use that magic as a way of evoking the nature of literary creation. In the earlier comedy it is an unruly force, creating unexpected events and ultimately providing a genial corrective to our confidence, and the Duke's confidence, in the primacy of reason and the quotidian. In *The Tempest* magic is under control, and unruliness and irrepressibility in the play may result from the audience and characters resisting the source of that control, Prospero. Hence when this play too includes a speculation on the nature of dramatic action, it is telling that it comes from Prospero, and that it applies not to the whole of the action, but to an inset masque arranged by the exiled Duke:

> You do look, my son, in a moved sort,
> As if you were dismayed. Be cheerful, sir.
> Our revels now are ended. These our actors,
> As I foretold you, were all spirits, and
> Are melted into air, into thin air;
> And like the baseless fabric of this vision,
> The cloud-capped towers, the gorgeous palaces,
> The solemn temples, the great globe itself,
> Yea, all which it inherit, shall dissolve;
> And, like this insubstantial pageant faded,
> Leave not a rack behind. We are such stuff
> As dreams are made on, and our little life
> Is rounded with a sleep. Sir, I am vexed,
> Bear with my weakness. My old brain is troubled.
> Be not disturbed with my infirmity.

(4.1.146–60)

Although this is in many ways a vital speech that reverberates outwards from its context, the audience has a great deal of imaginative space around it. It is started and ended with descriptions of perturbation: Prospero alleges that Ferdinand is 'in a moved sort', but at both ends of his speech it is the Duke himself who is 'troubled'. As has already been observed, Ferdinand seems less bothered by the apparitions than the Duke seems to think. Indeed, earlier in the scene he quickly guesses, and himself asserts, that the actors are spirits—Prospero's tone of comfort here ('As I foretold you') is spurious. These things would tend against the importance and extractability of the speech, but that is not what has happened in the reception of Shakespeare. This speech has been monumentalized, appearing on the poet's monument in Westminster Abbey. Its meaning has been treated as if it is a summary of the whole experience of drama, and yet in context it is delivering obvious reassurances to a listener who does not need them. This is a final example of the subtle yet persistent way in which Shakespeare's late work revisits the themes of his early work, and a final parallel to the way he incorporates a search for certainty and meaning and also the problems attending such a search. None of the profundity is lost, and yet the irony gathers.

It is not possible to do more here than give a few snapshots of the late plays' relationships with earlier works. This book's attempt to discern and explore their special characteristics should not obscure wider affinities. Shakespeare revisits central features of earlier plays and there seems to be at least one typical ratio in these revisions, with the later plays offering room for thought outside the pre-existing frameworks. This suggests that Shakespeare had a sense of the present and past of his literary career—that while he did not necessarily think of these plays as his last, he thought of them as later than previous work in more than just a chronological sense. This is consistent with the emphasis of Chapters 2–5, where a distinctive set of 'late' strategies was identified. However, this chapter also continues the work of the preceding one on Middleton and Fletcher, in that it suggests a less strategic Shakespeare and a less distinct body of late work. The continuities and affinities explored here, alongside the collaborative and wider cultural aspects of late Shakespeare explored in the preceding sections, warn against being too categorical about the late work's identity, given that it evidently participates in broader currents in Shakespeare's work and beyond. The two images of Shakespeare's later work—a distinct and self-aware phenomenon, or a product of its time that subsequent canonization has rarefied—need to be held in balance because, in effect, they are both true.

Further Reading

The classic studies of Shakespeare's late work remain suggestive: see in particular E. M. W. Tillyard, *Shakespeare's Last Plays* (London: Chatto & Windus, 1958), Derek Traversi, *Shakespeare: The Last Phase* (London: Hollis & Carter, 1954), and G. Wilson Knight, *The Crown of Life: Essays in Interpretation of Shakespeare's Final Plays* (London: Methuen, 1947). There are many approaches and assumptions in evidence that are not shared by the present study, but several key ones that are. Of more recent books on late Shakespeare, Robert M. Adams, *Shakespeare: The Four Romances* (New York: Norton, 1989) and Simon Palfrey, *Late Shakespeare: A New World of Words* (Oxford: Oxford University Press, 1997) offer arresting and contrasting interpretations.

A deeper understanding of the late work is aided by a deeper understanding of romance. Gillian Beer, *The Romance*, Critical Idiom Series (London: Methuen, 1970) remains a useful introduction. Howard Felperin, *Shakespearean Romance* (Princeton: Princeton University Press, 1972) and Helen Cooper, *The English Romance in Time: Transforming Motifs from Geoffrey of Monmouth to the Death of Shakespeare* (Oxford: Oxford University Press, 2004) connect Shakespeare with the tradition. Patricia Parker, *Inescapable Romance: Studies in the Poetics of a Mode* (Princeton: Princeton University Press, 1979) is an insightful analysis of romance's tendency towards deferral. Lawrence Danson, *Shakespeare's Dramatic Genres* (Oxford: Oxford University Press, 2000) is a very useful introduction to genre in the period more generally.

A book of this size cannot hope to do justice to every aspect of such rich works, nor to their critics. Thus it would be very instructive to follow it up by reading one or more collections of different essays. Kiernan Ryan (ed.), *Shakespeare's Last Plays* (London: Longman, 1999) and Alison Thorne (ed.), *Shakespeare's Romances*, New Casebook (Basingstoke: Palgrave Macmillan, 2003) are both ideal for the purpose. More diversity of approaches can be found in Jennifer Richards and James Knowles (eds.), *Shakespeare's Late Works: New Readings* (Edinburgh: Edinburgh University Press, 1999) and Carol McGinnis Kay and Henry E. Jacobs (eds.), *Shakespeare's Romances Reconsidered* (Lincoln: University of Nebraska Press, 1978). See also Gordon McMullan and Jonathan Hope (eds.), *The Politics of Tragicomedy: Shakespeare and After* (London and New York: Routledge, 1992) and Roger Warren, *Staging Shakespeare's Late Plays* (Oxford: Oxford University Press, 1990), both of which tackle areas which have been relatively under-explored in this book.

Shakespeare's Late Work advances an image of Shakespeare as an author that is derived from some brilliant and very diverse recent criticism. Brian Vickers, *Shakespeare, Co-Author: A Historical Study of Five Collaborative Plays* (Oxford: Oxford University Press, 2004) makes a compelling case; Jeffrey Masten, *Textual Intercourse: Collaboration, Authorship, and Sexualities in Renaissance Drama* (Cambridge: Cambridge University Press, 1997) is very different indeed in its treatment of collaboration once it is identified and restored to view. Graham Bradshaw, *Shakespeare's Scepticism* (Brighton: Harvester, 1987) remains a landmark in treating Shakespeare as an unusual kind of philosopher. Anne Righter (Barton), *Shakespeare and the Idea of the Play* (London: Penguin, 1962) is an excellent introduction to what can become a bit of a critical cliché; see also several essays in Anne Barton (same person), *Essays, Mainly Shakespearean* (Cambridge: Cambridge University Press, 1994). John Jones, *Shakespeare at Work* (Oxford: Oxford University Press, 2000) and Tiffany Stern, *Making Shakespeare: From Stage to Page* (London: Routledge, 2004) in different ways develop a rich sense of how the written works that survive relate to the stage on which they were performed. Lukas Erne, *Shakespeare as Literary Dramatist* (Cambridge: Cambridge University Press, 2003) and Patrick Cheney, *Shakespeare, National Poet-Playwright* (Cambridge: Cambridge University Press, 2004) develop ideas that Shakespeare thought about his career more closely than the traditional image of the natural genius would have us believe.

Particular topics tackled in the preceding chapters are elaborated elsewhere. On the emblematic connection of time and truth, see T. Fabiny, 'Veritas Filia Temporis. The Iconography of Time and Truth and Shakespeare', *Acta Universitatis Szegedensis De Attila József Nominatae Papers in English and American Studies*, 3 (1984), 215–71, and Debbie L. Barrett, 'Pericles, Social Redemption, and the Iconography of "Veritas Temporis Filia"', *Shakespeare Yearbook*, 2 (1991), 77–94. See also *Henry VIII*, ed. McMullan, 67–70. Alexandra Walsham, *Providence in Early Modern England* (Oxford University Press, 1999) explores the cultural history of a central concept.

Pauline Kiernan, *Shakespeare's Theory of Drama* (Cambridge: Cambridge University Press, 1996) is a fascinating analysis of how Shakespeare incorporates in his plays a theory and defence of drama as a distinct and special way in which to tell stories. With close attention to Shakespeare's interest in Ovid's *Metamorphoses* she explores how the body and its capacity to change (two things evidently at issue in these plays) often come to the fore. An important essay relating to the 'Seeing is Believing' chapter is Anne Barton,

'"Enter Mariners, wet": Realism in Shakespeare's Last Plays', in *Essays, Mainly Shakespearean*, 182–203.

A key work in orienting the late work within political contexts is David Bergeron, *Shakespeare's Romances and the Royal Family* (Lawrence: University of Kansas Press, 1985). Studies of *The Tempest* have explored its colonial dynamics to good effect: Paul Brown, '"This Thing of Darkness I Acknowledge Mine": *The Tempest* and the Discourses of Colonialism', in Jonathan Dollimore and Alan Sinfield (eds.), *Political Shakespeare: New Essays in Cultural Materialism* (Manchester: Manchester University Press, 1985), 48–71, and Peter Hulme and William Sherman (eds.), *The Tempest and its Travels* (London: Reaktion, 2000). On the relationship between *The Tempest* and travel writing, see Charles Frey, '*The Tempest* and the New World', *Shakespeare Quarterly*, 30 (1979), 29–41. David Norbrook, '"What Cares these Roarers for the Name of King?": Language and Utopia in *The Tempest*', in Kiernan Ryan (ed.), *Shakespeare's Last Plays* (London: Longman, 1999), 245–78; reprinted from Gordon McMullan and Jonathan Hope (eds.), *The Politics of Tragicomedy: Shakespeare and After* (London and New York: Routledge, 1992) and Constance Jordan, *Shakespeare's Monarchies: Ruler and Subject in the Romances* (Ithaca: Cornell University Press, 1997) read the plays as works interested in the theory and practice of royal power. Ros King's *'Cymbeline': Constructions of Britain* (Aldershot: Ashgate, 2004) is an important study of that play's connections with King James's project to unite Britain.

Questions of text and authorship are tackled in editions of the plays but also in key works of criticism. In the first chapter the question of the revision of *King Lear* comes to the fore. Among landmarks of the 1980s, when the revision theory began to gain acceptance, see Gary Taylor and Michael Warren (eds.), *The Division of the Kingdoms: Shakespeare's Two Versions of 'King Lear'* (Oxford: Clarendon Press, 1983) and Steven Urkowitz, *Shakespeare's Revision of 'King Lear'* (Princeton: Princeton University Press, 1980). In the 1990s editors of *Lear* reflected this change in thinking. The New Cambridge *Tragedy of King Lear*, ed. Jay L. Halio (Cambridge: Cambridge University Press, 1992) is a Folio-based text which puts Quarto-only passages in an appendix. (Cambridge published *The First Quarto of King Lear*, ed. Jay L. Halio, in 1992, while Oxford published *The History of King Lear*, ed. Stanley Wells, and based on Gary Taylor's text for the collected works, in 2000.) A bold solution can be found in the Arden 3rd series *King Lear*, ed. R. A. Foakes (Walton-on-Thames: Thomas Nelson, 1997). Foakes includes all Q-only and F-only passages, in general preferring F when a choice becomes necessary, but marks diverging readings by peppering the text with superscript 'Q' and 'F'.

The relationships between Shakespeare and his contemporaries, tackled in Chapter 6, have been illuminated by scholars of the Middleton and

Fletcher canons. David J. Lake, *The Canon of Thomas Middleton's Plays: Internal Evidence for the Major Problems of Authorship* (Cambridge: Cambridge University Press, 1975), MacDonald P. Jackson, *Studies in Attribution: Middleton and Shakespeare*, Salzburg Studies in English Literature: Jacobean Studies (Salzburg, 1979), and R. V. Holdsworth, 'Middleton and Shakespeare' (unpublished Ph.D. dissertation, University of Manchester, 1982) are key studies. There is an interesting but inconclusive exchange between two scholars as to whether Shakespeare might have been responsible for some additions made to *The Second Maiden's Tragedy* on slips of paper inserted into the manuscript. See Eric Rasmussen, 'Shakespeare's Hand in *The Second Maiden's Tragedy*', *Shakespeare Quarterly*, 40 (1989), 1–26, MacDonald P. Jackson, 'The Additions to *The Second Maiden's Tragedy*: Shakespeare's or Middleton's?', *Shakespeare Quarterly*, 41 (1990), 402–5, and Eric Rasmussen, 'Reply to MacDonald P. Jackson', *Shakespeare Quarterly*, 41 (1990), 406–7. Relations with Fletcher have been explored by Lee Bliss, 'Three Plays in One: Shakespeare and *Philaster*', *Medieval and Renaissance Drama in England*, 2 (1985), 153–70, and Daniel Morley McKeithan, *The Debt to Shakespeare in the Beaumont and Fletcher Plays* (New York: Gardiner Press, 1970), among others.

Frank Kermode, *Shakespeare's Language* (Harmondsworth: Penguin, 2000) is one of a number of scholarly accounts of the language of Shakespeare's late work. Among the landmarks in language criticism are: Maurice Hunt, *Shakespeare's Romance of the Word* (London: Associated University Presses, 1990), Molly Mahood, *Shakespeare's Wordplay* (London, 1957), esp. 146–63, and two essays in Philip Edwards, Inga-Stina Ewbank, and G. K. Hunter (eds.), *Shakespeare's Styles: Essays in Honour of Kenneth Muir* (Cambridge: Cambridge University Press, 1980): Anne Barton, 'Leontes and the Spider: Language and Speaker in Shakespeare's Last Plays', and Inga-Stina Ewbank, '"My Name is Marina": The Language of Recognition'. See also Anne Barton, 'Shakespeare and the Limits of Language', *Shakespeare Survey*, 24 (1971), 19–30. Both the Barton essays can be found in *Essays, Mainly Shakespearean*. See also Howard Felperin, '"Tongue-tied, our Queen?": The Deconstruction of Presence in *The Winter's Tale*', in Kiernan Ryan (ed.), *Shakespeare's Last Plays* (London: Longman, 1999), 187–205; reprinted from Patricia Parker and Geoffrey Hartman (eds.), *Shakespeare and the Question of Theory* (London: Methuen, 1985).

Finally, Claire Colebrook, *Irony*, New Critical Idiom Series (London: Routledge, 2004) is an excellent introduction to a central topic in this book.

| *Notes*

CHAPTER I

1. E. M. W. Tillyard, *Shakespeare's Last Plays* (London: Chatto & Windus, 1938), 22.
2. Derek Traversi, *Shakespeare: The Last Phase* (London: Hollis & Carter, 1954), 272.
3. Fletcher used the word in the preface of his play *The Faithful Shepherdess* (London, 1610), the first substantial English theorization. For more information on tragicomedy, see Further Reading.
4. For the tradition of romance, and Shakespeare's place in it, see Further Reading.
5. Patricia Parker, *Inescapable Romance: Studies in the Poetics of a Mode* (Princeton: Princeton University Press, 1979).
6. Northrop Frye, *The Secular Scripture: A Study of the Structure of Romance* (Cambridge, Mass.: Harvard University Press, 1976), 183.
7. See Dilwyn Knox, *Ironia: Medieval and Renaissance Ideas on Irony* (Leiden: E. J. Brill, 1989), 97–101.
8. Claire Colebrook, *Irony*, New Critical Idiom Series (London: Routledge, 2004). This book gives an excellent account of ironic thought from Plato to postmodernism.
9. Many of Schlegel's key ideas, in theory and practice, are in *Philosophical Fragments*, trans. Peter Firchow (Minneapolis: University of Minnesota Press, 1991).
10. See D. C. Muecke, *Irony and the Ironic* (London: Methuen, 1980), 18–27. See Steven E. Alford, *Irony and the Logic of the English Romantic Imagination* (New York: Peter Lang, 1984).
11. Georg Lukács, *The Theory of the Novel*, trans. Anna Bostock (London: Merlin, 1971).
12. See Richard H. Popkin, *The History of Scepticism from Erasmus to Spinoza* (Berkeley and Los Angeles: University of California Press, 1979), esp. 42–65 on Montaigne.
13. Graham Bradshaw, *Shakespeare's Scepticism* (Brighton: Harvester, 1987), 94.

14. Anne Righter, *Shakespeare and the Idea of the Play* (London: Penguin, 1962).

15. Robert Boies Sharpe, *Irony in the Drama: An Essay on Impersonation, Shock, and Catharsis* (Chapel Hill: University of North Carolina Press, 1989), 53.

16. Ibid. 80.

17. David Bevington, 'Irony and its Interrelatedness in Shakespeare', in Philip H. Highfill, Jr. (ed.), *Shakespeare's Craft: Eight Lectures* (Carbondale: Southern Illinois University Press, 1985), 1–23, p. 23.

18. Brian Vickers, *Shakespeare, Co-Author: A Historical Study of Five Collaborative Plays* (Oxford: Oxford University Press, 2004).

19. Jonathan Hope, *The Authorship of Shakespeare's Plays: A Socio-Linguistic Study* (Cambridge: Cambridge University Press, 1994), 152. See also MacDonald P. Jackson, *Defining Shakespeare: 'Pericles' as Test Case* (Oxford: Oxford University Press, 2003).

20. Vickers, *Shakespeare, Co-Author*, 433–500.

21. *Henry VIII*, ed. Gordon McMullan (London: Thomson Learning, 2000), 180–99.

22. See Vickers, *Shakespeare, Co-Author*, 397–402; also 506–41, an appendix defending the notion of the author in the period. Foucault's essay is 'What Is an Author?', in Josué V. Harari (ed.), *Textual Strategies: Perspectives in Post-Structuralist Criticism* (Ithaca, NY: Cornell University Press, 1979), 141–60. Foucault's essay does indeed make a sweeping and highly questionable generalization about the lack of a conception of authorship before the Enlightenment. Vickers's list of renaissance and classical examples wins the argument at a number of levels, but Foucault's essay can survive, as a suggestive challenge to retrospective extrapolation of our own idea of authorship into periods where the idea was not so stable.

23. Jeffrey Masten, *Textual Intercourse: Collaboration, Authorship, and Sexualities in Renaissance Drama* (Cambridge: Cambridge University Press, 1997).

24. G. Wilson Knight, *The Crown of Life: Essays in Interpretation of Shakespeare's Final Plays* (London: Methuen, 1946), 256.

25. Robert M. Adams, *Shakespeare: The Four Romances* (New York: Norton, 1989), 178. The Oxford Shakespeare interprets contemporary references to the play as *All Is True* as evidence of its original title; despite my following the Oxford text it will be referred to by its more familiar title in this book. *Henry VIII*, ed. McMullan, 93–120, and more generally in the Introduction, offers a nuanced account of truth in the play, and makes a strong case for considering the play alongside other late Shakespearian works, especially *The Winter's Tale*.

26. For the story of the Queen of Sheba and her reverence for Solomon's wisdom, see 1 Kings 10: 1–13. It is tantalizing to wonder what readers of *Henry VIII* are to do with the fact that the biblical Queen sought wisdom not in itself, but in a man.

27. See *The Two Noble Kinsmen*, ed. Lois Potter (Walton-on-Thames: Thomas Nelson, 1997), 35–7, on the possible connections between the play and the wedding celebrations.

28. Helen Cooper, *The English Romance in Time: Transforming Motifs from Geoffrey of Monmouth to the Death of Shakespeare* (Oxford: Oxford University Press, 2004), 375.

29. See *The Tempest*, ed. Stephen Orgel (Oxford: Oxford University Press, 1987), 56–61. See also S. Wells and G. Taylor, *William Shakespeare: A Textual Companion* (Oxford: Clarendon Press, 1987), 20–2, on Ralph Crane being the probable scribe of the manuscripts on which the Folio *Tempest*, *Winter's Tale*, and *Cymbeline* were based, and on his characteristic interventions. Detailed stage directions were one of his hallmarks. Another theatre company scribe of the period, Mr Knight, was probably responsible for the manuscript on which the 1634 quarto of *The Two Noble Kinsmen* was based, and he also tended to write detailed stage directions—on which see Wells and Taylor, *Textual Companion*, 22–3.

30. Orgel, 97.

31. See John Freehafer, '*Cardenio*, by Shakespeare and Fletcher', *PMLA*, 84 (1969), 501–13, for the salient facts outlined below.

32. The translation is *The History of the Valorous and Wittie Knight-Errant, Don-Quixote of the Mancha Translated out of the Spanish*, trans. Thomas Shelton (London, 1612). Its preface mentions that the work was written a few years earlier, so it would not require inordinate alacrity on behalf of Fletcher and Shakespeare to feel its influence.

33. Jonathan Bate, *The Genius of Shakespeare* (London: Picador, 1997), 76–82. Bate is another key source of the facts outlined in this section. See also Stephen Kukowski, 'The Hand of John Fletcher in *Double Falsehood*', *Shakespeare Survey*, 43 (1991), 81–9.

34. Lewis Theobald, *Double Falshood; or, The Distrest Lovers* (London, 1728), 1.3.8–14.

35. See *Textual Companion*, 93–143. Wells and Taylor order the key plays as follows: *Pericles* (1607), *Coriolanus* (1608), *The Winter's Tale* (1609), the revised Folio *King Lear* (1610), on which more below, *Cymbeline* (1610), *The Tempest* (1611), the lost *Cardenio* (1612–13), *All Is True/Henry VIII* (1613), *The Two Noble Kinsmen* (1613–14). These are necessarily subtle and debatable judgements. The idea that *Pericles* is the first step in a new direction does not depend on it following *Coriolanus*—creative phases

(if that is what is in evidence) can overlap. The order of *Cymbeline* and *The Winter's Tale* is likewise not critical: in the discussions below the important thing will be that these were the two plays—with many things, including the time of composition, closely entwined—that immediately preceded *The Tempest*.

36. See Raphael Lyne, 'Shakespeare, Plautus, and the Discovery of New Comic Space', in Charles Martindale and A. B. Taylor (eds.), *Shakespeare and the Classics* (Cambridge: Cambridge University Press, 2004), 120–38.

37. Forman's entries on Shakespeare plays can be found in numerous editions and anthologies, e.g. in G. Blakemore Evans (ed.), *The Riverside Shakespeare*, 2nd edn. (Boston: Houghton Mifflin, 1997), 1841–2. On the repertory system, see Andrew Gurr, *The Shakespearian Stage 1574–1642*, 3rd edn. (Cambridge: Cambridge University Press, 1992), 106–14.

38. This subject has attracted much insightful criticism, for which see Further Reading.

39. John Jones, *Shakespeare at Work* (Oxford: Oxford University Press, 2000).

40. Ibid. 64–83.

41. A. C. Bradley, *Shakespearian Tragedy* (London: Macmillan, 1994), 291.

42. See *The Complete Poems and Sonnets*, ed. Colin Burrow (Oxford: Oxford University Press, 2002), 103–6.

CHAPTER 2

1. Samuel Taylor Coleridge, *Biographia Literaria*, 2 vols., ed. James Engell and W. Jackson Bate, *The Collected Works of Samuel Taylor Coleridge*, no. 7 (Princeton: Princeton University Press, 1983), ii. 6.

2. *Hamlet*, 3.2.94–102.

3. See S. Wells and G. Taylor, *Willliam Shakespeare: A Textual Companion* (Oxford: Clarendon Press, 1987), 553, on both 'vile' and 'awry'. Retaining F's 'wild[e]' is said to be 'defensible' but appearances of the phrase 'vile world' elsewhere strengthen the case for emendation.

4. See Anne Barton, '"Enter Mariners, wet": Realism in Shakespeare's Last Plays', in *Essays, Mainly Shakespearean* (Cambridge: Cambridge University Press, 1994), 182–203.

5. *Inigo Jones: The Theatre of the Stuart Court*, ed. Stephen Orgel and Roy Strong, 2 vols. (Berkeley and Los Angeles: University of California Press, 1973), is a glorious anthology of masque designs.

6. Thomas Heywood, *The Golden Age* (London, 1611).

7. See James Knowles, 'Insubstantial Pageants: *The Tempest* and Masquing Culture', in Jennifer Richards and James Knowles (eds.), *Shakespeare's Late Plays: New Readings* (Edinburgh: Edinburgh University Press, 1999), 108–23. See also Michael Bristol, 'Theatre and Popular Culture', in John

D. Cox and David Scott Kastan (eds.), *A New History of Early English Drama* (New York: Columbia University Press, 1997), 231–48.

8. Leah S. Marcus, '*Cymbeline* and the Unease of Topicality', in Kiernan Ryan (ed.), *Shakespeare's Last Plays* (London: Longman, 1999), 134–68.

9. Frank Kermode, *Shakespeare's Language* (Harmondsworth: Penguin, 2000), 284–300, discusses the characteristic speech styles of both Caliban and Ariel.

10. *Textual Companion*, 614–15.

CHAPTER 3

1. It bears the title *The late, and much admired play, called Pericles, Prince of Tyre … By William Shakespeare* (London, 1609). George Wilkins published his prose fiction *The Painful Adventures of Pericles Prince of Tyre* in 1608. This work has been treated as a source for *Pericles* and as a work based on *Pericles*. Selections can be found in editions of *Pericles* and in G. Bullough (ed.), *Narrative and Dramatic Sources of Shakespeare* (London: Routledge & Kegan Paul, 1966), vi. 492–546. See S. Wells and G. Taylor, *William Shakespeare: A Textual Companion* (Oxford: Clarendon Press, 1987), 556–60, for the Oxford conclusions that it derived from *Pericles* in the theatre, and that the 1609 Q *Pericles* was a memorial reconstruction with weak points and strong points. The Oxford text of *Pericles*, quoted here, results from a very unusual editorial practice. The two key premisses are (1) that Q is so clearly aberrant, especially in Acts 1 and 2, that it requires considerable emendation, and (2) that *Painful Adventures* is at times a more reliable report of the theatre text than Q. Thus Gary Taylor and collaborator MacDonald P. Jackson offer a 'reconstruction' of *Pericles* in which they feel free to change Q considerably when there is precedent in *Painful Adventures*. This text is the basis of Roger Warren's edition of the play (Oxford: Oxford University Press, 2004). Suzanne Gossett's Arden edition (London: Thomson Learning, 2004) accepts these premisses but emends the text less radically. The edition of Antony Hammond and Doreen Delvecchio (Cambridge: Cambridge University Press, 1998) asserts instead the integrity of the maligned Q as a text and a performable play, and emends it as little as possible.

2. See Terence Cave, *Recognitions: A Study in Poetics* (Oxford: Oxford University Press, 1988), esp. 276–82 on *Twelfth Night*.

3. Ibid. 286–92.

4. *Textual Companion*, 587.

5. See ibid. 588, on all the editorial changes in this passage.

6. E. K. Chambers, *William Shakespeare: A Study of Facts and Problems*, 2 vols. (Oxford: Clarendon Press, 1930), i. 85–6.

7. Claire Preston, 'The Emblematic Structure of *Pericles*', *Word and Image*, 8 (1992), 21–38.

8. F. D. Hoeniger, 'Gower and Shakespeare in *Pericles*', *Shakespeare Quarterly*, 33 (1982), 461–79.

9. *Pericles*, ed. F. D. Hoeniger (London: Methuen, 1963), pp. lxxxviii–xci.

10. *Textual Companion*, 574.

11. Ibid. 561.

12. See ibid. 576, on various changes in this speech. Q has 'green' for 'grave' in line 66, and 'grave' for 'tomb' in line 68. In line 71 Q has 'as a lasting' for 'but a ceaseless'. The Oxford edition's theory of the text—a patched-together memorial reconstruction—validates these alterations, which do indeed produce a more coherent version.

13. It is perhaps no coincidence that Paulina's name evokes that of St Paul, the author of key epistles in the New Testament in which the foundations of much Christian theology, and the theory of grace in particular, are found. Despite the curious authority Paulina assumes in judging the King's spiritual state, it does not seem as if this gathers into a distinct theological point.

14. Portia's famous speech on mercy in *The Merchant of Venice* 4.1.181–4. shows this pattern of thought is not seen only in the late plays: 'The quality of mercy is not strained. | It droppeth as the gentle rain from heaven | Upon the place beneath. It is twice blest: | It blesseth him that gives, and him that takes.' The affinity between this and the examples from the romances is obvious, but their concentration and pivotal positioning in the late plays are notable.

15. Quotations from the Geneva Bible, spelling modernized.

16. John Davies, *The Holy Roode or Christes Cross* (London, 1609), 1906–11.

17. John Davies, 'A Confession of a Sinner', 57–60, in *The Muses Sacrifice* (London, 1612).

18. For Davies's biography, see P. J. Finkelpearl, 'Davies, John (1564/5–1618)', *Oxford Dictionary of National Biography*, Oxford University Press, 2004 [<http://www. oxforddnb.com/view/article/7244>, accessed 18 July 2005]. Richard Wilson, *Secret Shakespeare: Studies in Theatre, Religion, and Resistance* (Manchester: Manchester University Press, 2004), sets out the case for Shakespeare's Catholicism.

CHAPTER 4

1. Cyrus Hoy, 'Fathers and Daughters in Shakespeare's Romances', in Carol McGinnis Kay and Henry E. Jacobs (eds.), *Shakespeare's Romances Reconsidered* (Lincoln: University of Nebraska Press, 1978), 84.

2. Richard McCabe, *Incest, Drama, and Nature's Law 1550–1700* (Cambridge: Cambridge University Press, 1993), 179.

3. Coppélia Kahn, 'The Providential Tempest and the Shakespearian Family', in Coppélia Kahn and Murray M. Schwartz (eds.), *Representing Shakespeare: New Psychoanalytic Essays* (Baltimore: Johns Hopkins University Press, 1980), 217–32, p. 230.

4. See the classic essay by Nevill Coghill, 'Six Points of Stage-Craft in *The Winter's Tale*', *Shakespeare Survey*, 11 (1958), 31–41, reprinted in Kenneth Muir (ed.), *The Winter's Tale: A Casebook* (London: Macmillan, 1968), 198–213.

5. David Sundelson, *Shakespeare's Restorations of the Father* (New Brunswick, NJ: Rutgers University Press, 1983).

6. Kahn, 'The Providential Tempest and the Shakespearian Family', 229.

7. Janet Adelman, *Suffocating Mothers: Fantasies of Maternal Origin in Shakespeare's Plays, Hamlet to The Tempest* (New York: Routledge, 1992), 194.

8. Marjorie Garber, *Coming of Age in Shakespeare* (London: Methuen, 1997), 32–4.

9. J. I. M. Stewart, *Character and Motive in Shakespeare: Some Recent Appraisals Examined* (London: Longman, 1949), 30–7.

10. S. Wells and G. Taylor, *William Shakespeare: A Textual Companion* (Oxford: Clarendon Press, 1987), 575.

11. Ann Thompson, *Shakespeare's Chaucer: A Study in Literary Origins* (Liverpool: Liverpool University Press, 1978), 166–215.

12. See Frank Kermode, *Shakespeare's Language* (Harmondsworth: Penguin, 2000), 244–5, and Further Reading.

CHAPTER 5

1. Northrop Frye, *The Secular Scripture: A Study of the Structure of Romance* (Cambridge, Mass.: Harvard University Press), 161.

2. Annabel Patterson, *Shakespeare and the Popular Voice* (Oxford: Basil Blackwell, 1989), 120–53, explores popular rebellion in *Coriolanus*. Whereas some critics find that Shakespeare is disdainful about mob dynamics, Patterson argues that, in giving them political representation and considerable

effectiveness in the political landscape of the play, he is exploring radical possibilities.

3. E. M. W. Tillyard, *The Elizabethan World-Picture* (London: Chatto & Windus, 1943), is often cited as the source of a debilitating idea that Elizabethans all saw the world in one ordered way. This is clearly wrong for Shakespeare, but it is also not quite fair on Tillyard, whose book does describe the political use of such ideas, and the changes that accompanied them, rather than just being narrowly descriptive.

4. David Bergeron, *Shakespeare's Romances and the Royal Family* (Lawrence: University of Kansas Press, 1985), esp. 157–78.

5. Ibid. 160. It has already been noted that Hermione does not revive in *Pandosto*; nor does she in Simon Forman's description of seeing the play.

6. See David Norbrook, ' "What Cares these Roarers for the Name of King?": Language and Utopia in *The Tempest*', in Kiernan Ryan (ed.), *Shakespeare's Last Plays* (London: Longman, 1999), 245–78.

7. S. Wells and G. Taylor, *William Shakespeare: A Textual Companion* (Oxford: Clarendon Press, 1987), 614. Theobald, in 1733, was the first editor of Shakespeare to reallocate the speech, though it was done in effect by Dryden and Davenant in their Restoration adaptation *The Tempest; or, The Enchanted Island* (1667).

8. Sir Francis Bacon, *The Essayes or Counsels, Civill or Morall*, ed. Michael Kiernan (Oxford: Clarendon Press, 1985), 108 (modernized).

9. Stephen Greenblatt recognizes the limits of Prospero's power in his chapter 'Martial Law in the Land of Cockaigne', *Shakespearian Negotiations: The Circulation of Social Energy in Renaissance England* (Oxford: Oxford University Press, 1988), 129–63. His central argument is that Prospero practises a strategy of 'salutary anxiety' also evident in the power and punishment system of renaissance England. This involves raising the level of tension in someone you wish to educate thereby. It works on Ferdinand, but the cases of Caliban and Antonio show that 'the strategy of salutary anxiety cannot remake the inner life of everyone' (146).

10. Patterson, *Shakespeare and the Popular Voice*, 159.

11. Simon Palfrey, *Late Shakespeare: A New World of Words* (Oxford: Oxford University Press, 1997).

CHAPTER 6

1. David L. Frost, *The School of Shakespeare: The Influence of Shakespeare on English Drama 1600–1642* (Cambridge: Cambridge University Press, 1968), 23–76.

2. Ibid. 209–45.

3. On questions of authorship, see Further Reading.

4. Tiffany Stern, *Making Shakespeare: From Stage to Page* (London: Routledge, 2004), 32–3 on *Macbeth* as a court performance, and 60–1 on the date of additions by Middleton. See also Stephen Orgel, '*Macbeth* and the Antic Round', *Shakespeare Survey*, 52 (1999), 143–53.

5. James wrote *Daemonologie* (Edinburgh, 1597) while King of Scotland.

6. See Brian Vickers, *Shakespeare, Co-Author: A Historical Study of Five Collaborative Plays* (Oxford: Oxford University Press, 2004), 244–90.

7. *Timon of Athens*, ed. John Jowett (Oxford: Oxford University Press, 2004), 151. Jowett (pp. 3–9) dates the play 1604–6, and most likely early in 1606.

8. See S. Wells and G. Taylor, *William Shakespeare: A Textual Companion* (Oxford: Clarendon Press, 1987), 501. The lack of evidence of contemporary performances is suggestive but far from conclusive; the Oxford editors conclude that *Timon* would have been printed later in the Folio, 'or not at all'.

9. *The Second Maiden's Tragedy*, ed. Anne Lancashire, Revels Plays edn. (Manchester: Manchester University Press, 1978), 5.2.81–6.

10. *The Knight of the Burning Pestle*, in *The Dramatic Works in the Beaumont and Fletcher Canon*, general ed. Fredson Bowers, ii (Cambridge: Cambridge University Press, 1970), Act 5 lines 1–9, 19–30, spelling modernized.

11. *The Woman's Prize; or The Tamer Tamed*, in *The Dramatic Works in the Beaumont and Fletcher Canon*, iv (1979), 1.1.13–38.

12. See two essays in Charles Frey (ed.), *Shakespeare, Fletcher, and the Two Noble Kinsmen* (Columbia: University of Missouri Press, 1989)—Charles Frey, 31–44, and Donald Hedrick, 45–77.

13. *The Sea Voyage*, in *The Dramatic Works in the Beaumont and Fletcher Canon*, ix (1994), 1.1.1–11, 17–26.

14. Fletcher's *Maid's Tragedy* also incorporates elements of *Hamlet*, in particular an intense brother–sister 'closet scene'.

15. *Philaster*, in *The Dramatic Works in the Beaumont and Fletcher Canon*, i (1966), 5.3.19–33.

16. Andrew Gurr, in his Revels Plays edn. of *Philaster* (London: Methuen, 1969), pp. lxii–lxiv, argues that the play's gods are always depicted as benign and that it has a benevolent structure overall. It is indeed wrong to see the final reversal as an aberration without foundation in the play. Nevertheless it can still be argued that the quality of the surprise is unlike anything in Shakespeare—not least because it is so unironic.

17. *A King and No King*, in *The Dramatic Works in the Beaumont and Fletcher Canon*, ii (1970), 5.4.63–4, 108, 115–17.

18. Verna A. Foster, *The Name and Nature of Tragicomedy* (Aldershot: Ashgate, 2004), 72.

CHAPTER 7

1. William Strachey's description of a ship being blown off course, with its crew spending the winter in Bermuda, and falling into arguments, was written soon after the event in 1609, but not printed until 1625 (in *Purchas his Pilgrimes*, a compendium of travel writings). A number of Shakespeare's connections, such as the Earl of Southampton, were close to the Virginia Company and it is thus very likely that he could have seen the letter earlier.

2. It is interesting to note that these themes are central also to *Double Falshood* and to the story of Cardenio in *Don Quixote*.

3. E. M. W. Tillyard, *Shakespeare's Last Plays* (London: Chatto & Windus, 1958), *passim*.

4. S. Wells and G. Taylor, *William Shakespeare: A Textual Companion* (Oxford: Clarendon Press, 1987), 480.

5. See *A Midsummer Night's Dream*, ed. Peter Holland (Oxford: Oxford University Press, 1994), 257–65.